Voicing Vulnerable Bodies Living on the Edges

Queer Studies in Education

VOLUME 3

The titles published in this series are listed at *brill.com/queer*

Voicing Vulnerable Bodies Living on the Edges

The Autoethnography of a Transnational Mariposa

By

Juan A. Ríos Vega

BRILL

LEIDEN | BOSTON

Cover illustration: Photograph by Robert W. Nolan, ii

All chapters in this book have undergone peer review.

The Library of Congress Cataloging-in-Publication Data is available online at https://catalog.loc.gov

Typeface for the Latin, Greek, and Cyrillic scripts: "Brill". See and download: brill.com/brill-typeface.

ISSN 2773-0794
ISBN 978-90-04-71475-5 (paperback)
ISBN 978-90-04-71476-2 (hardback)
ISBN 978-90-04-71477-9 (e-book)
DOI 10.1163/9789004714779

No soy un marica disfrazado de poeta
No necesito disfraz
Aquí está mi cara
Hablo por mi diferencia
Defiendo lo que soy
Y no soy tan raro
Me apesta la injusticia ...

I'm not a fag disguised as a poet
I don't need a costume
here is my face
I speak for my difference
I defend what I am
And I'm not that weird
Injustice reeks of me ...

PEDRO LEMEBEL (2021, Manifiesto [Hablo por mi diferencia], p. 121. Loco afán. Crónicas de sidario)

∴

Contents

About the Author

Dr. Ríos earned a master of education in Curriculum and Teaching with Emphasis in English as a Second Language (ESL) from The University of North Carolina at Greensboro (2006) and received his doctorate in Philosophy in Educational Studies, Cultural Studies Concentration from The University of North Carolina at Greensboro (2014), and Women's and Gender Studies Certificate. His areas of research include Critical Race Theory, LatCrit Theory, Social Justice in Education, Multicultural Education, and Gender Studies. In 2015, he published his first book *Counterstorytelling Narratives of Latino Teenage Boys: From Vergüenza to Échale Ganas* (Peter Lang Publishing). In 2020, he published *High School Latinx Counternarratives: Experiences in School and Post-graduation* (Peter Lang Publishing). This book was selected as one of the 2021 Critics Choice Awards Books by the American Educational Studies Association (AESA). Currently, Dr. Ríos is an Associate Professor in the Department of Education, Counseling, and Leadership at Bradley University.

CHAPTER 1

Living on the Edges in Panama

Puedes pensar de mí, un común homosexual
O una reprimida puta, tú puedes ser un cielo
Y yo tu pájaro abreviado, un lingote
Vegetal asumido a tus guarniciones infinitas …

You can think of me, a common homosexual
Or a repressed whore, you can be a heaven
And I your abbreviated bird, an ingot
Assumed vegetable to your infinite garnishes …

> JAVIER ALVARADO (2013, La pintura al otro lado de la pared [pp. 97–100].
> Carta natal al país de los locos)

∴

I always knew that I was different. It was an everyday reminder from my older brother, my mom, my cousins, and my classmates. I grew up with a single mother and two siblings, a sister, and a brother. I was the youngest of the three, the one who looked and behaved like my mother, the opinionated, the talented, the smallest, and the *maricón*.[1] Being different in Latin American countries is not easy. From day one, individuals are supposed to follow strict gender expectations created by society and emphasized by religion. Society tells us when we are expected to like the opposite sex, when to start dating, when to get married, and when to have children. If we do not follow those expectations, we are in trouble, or our genders are questioned, literally, people ask you why?

When you are a boy raised by a single mother in a very traditional/catholic environment, it is very common to hear people saying that you turn gay due to a lack of a father figure. Most of the time, people believe that shit. Then I wonder, what happened to my brother? How he did not turn gay, like me? Or my husband who was raised by his two parents. Now, as an adult and scholar, I realize how society brainwashes individuals who, like me, do not follow their expectations.

Although I was a happy boy, I was afraid to be around other boys since they tended to bully (this word did not even exist when I was a child) me for not being masculine enough. By that time, those actions were probably called boys' games and were accepted as "normal." I still recall them with anger, like an open scar that will never be healed.

As a student K-12 in Panama's public school in the countryside, I always stood out for being the shortest, the skinniest, the most talented, and the most effeminate. I enjoyed being part of poetry, speech, drawing, and bulletin board contests. I loved to volunteer, to organize field trips, to participate in beauty pageant contests, and to decorate stages and floats. I was the typical *maricón*. Being the typical maricon made me vulnerable to being called homophobic slurs. I was *maricón, cueco*,[2] *pato*,[3] and sometimes called Juanita since the idea was that all gay men want to become women. The irony of this was that some of the boys who used to call me names ended up having sex with me when I was in middle school.

Writing and reflecting on this part of my life as a *maricón* has not been easy. I feel that since I was a child, I was sexually harassed by neighboring boys, male classmates, and older men (some of them used to be my mother's friends). Although I knew that I liked boys and had intercourse with some of them, I also felt attracted to girls. I guess that I did it to please my mom. I dated and had sex with a couple of girls in my neighborhood and at school. I dated a girl for over two years before I left my mom's house and moved to Panama City to pursue higher education. We had sex many times. I am so glad that she never got pregnant; otherwise, my story would be different today. After I finished college, I went back to the countryside to propose to her, but she told me that it was too late. She was already dating somebody else.

I started college in August 1989. Then in December of the same year, the U.S. government invaded Panama with the excuse to capture Manuel Antonio Noriega. The 1990s were terrible years for my country. While pursuing my college education, I had sex with other women. But I still felt attracted to other men. I liked being around a couple of my classmates who seemed to be very heterosexual, but I never said a word. I was afraid to be rejected or ridiculed.

I have always loved dancing. When I was a junior in college, I was going through a lot of stress. I wanted to move away from my relatives' house and become more independent, but I was afraid since I did not have enough money to survive on my own. I had a college scholarship and was already tutoring some students after school. A friend of mine, Manuela, suggested joining some non-academic groups on campus to release my stress and I did it. I joined a theater group and a dance troop. I had the most amazing experiences of my life. I met wonderful people and heard the most amazing stories. I learned that I guy in the theater group was dating an older guy, I met an older woman who asked for money every time we met, I met the theater instructor who had just arrived from Cuba with her Cuban husband, and I learned that one of the most outstanding theater directors of Panama had died of AIDS. Even though there were some other guys in this group that caught my attention, I never said a word. The theme of being a *maricón* was never discussed.

Unlike the theater group, the dance group was full of *maricónes*. They were all friendly and fun. They never talked to me about being gay or any gay topic. However, most of them already knew each other before I joined the group. One night after rehearsal, they invited me to eat pizza in an Italian restaurant very close to La 4 de Julio (July 4th Avenue), a famous avenue in Panama City for its nightlife of prostitution and travesties. My friends wanted to take me to a gay bar without telling me that it was a gay bar. I guess they wanted to confirm that I was gay too. I was curious and decided to join them. It was the most bizarre place that I had ever seen in my life. I saw women dancing with other women and men dancing with me. It was a cultural shock for me. I was shaking all over. However, things got worse when one of my friends asked me to dance with him. I rejected the offer right away. I could not understand how two people of the same gender would be dancing together. Then my friend told me that he had some feelings for me and that was it. I left that place as soon as I could. To my surprise, when I was outside waiting for a cab, some of my college friends (all of them women) saw me. They yelled my name and asked me to get in the cab, which I did. While in the car, they promised to take me to a better place. That night I learned that many of my friends in the car were lesbians. When I got to the gay disco called Le Garage, I realized that many of my friends at the university were also gay and I did not know. All of them hugged and kissed me. One of them told me that he always wanted to invite me to Le Garage, but he was afraid to do it. Since that night, I never stopped going to Le Garage on Fridays, Saturdays, and sometimes on Sundays since the drag shows were hilarious and well-known in the community. I had to share that most of these gay places were in hidden or dangerous places in the city. For instance, Le Garage was hidden behind deposit hangars. It was the 1990s; the pandemic of HIV/AIDS became a stigma in the LGBT community, and homosexuality was still legally punishable in Panama.

It was in Le Garage that I fell in love with another man for the first time. Ariel was also an impersonator who went by the name La Perla. We fell in love. But like most young gay guys, I wanted to explore more options and broke up with Ariel after a few months. Then, I dated a couple of guys who took advantage of me, stole my money, lived in my place for free, or told me countless lies.

In 1998, I was in my mid-20s. I was already teaching English in a high school in Panama City. I started dating Mauricio, a young and sexy guy. Mauricio was already 18 years old and had recently graduated from the same high school where I was teaching. Based on Panama's laws, Mauricio was already an adult. Mauricio and I had a secret love affair. We fell in love with each other. He was full of life and energy. Mauricio was an excellent folk dancer. He cared a lot about his mom and younger sister. After 3 years, I switched jobs to a private school. I wanted to make more money. Mauricio and I dated until I quit my job as a teacher in Panama and moved to the United States on August 1, 1999.

I kept in touch with Mauricio for over a year. We promised each other many things, especially to be loyal to each other. We picked our theme song. We cried like crazy the day I left my beloved country. Mauricio was still very young, with many dreams and goals to fulfill. He wanted to become a lawyer. Unfortunately, our relationship did not last long. Mauricio started dating other guys. He dropped out of college due to his finances and worked in different fast-food restaurants. Ariel and Mauricio became the only two guys with whom I fell in love while living in Panama. Sadly, both passed away. I was afraid to ask how and what caused their deaths. It is always believed that if you are a *maricón*, you will eventually die of AIDS, no matter what. It is like being a *maricón* marks your destiny as *sidoso* (HIV+).

As I mentioned earlier, I moved to the United States in 1999 to work as an exchange teacher in North Carolina. In the beginning, it was tough, as it is for any immigrant who moves to a place where issues of race, language, immigration, and class are so salient. At first, I lived with a roommate from Panama. Her name was Rosa (pseudonym). Rosa and I struggled to get along with each other at the beginning. She was a divorced woman with two daughters back in Panama. Rosa was used to being in control and making decisions for her family. However, I was used to being independent. In the beginning, I decided not to share with Rosa about my sexuality. I was afraid that she would reject me or start behaving differently. However, I started searching gay places in North Carolina until I found a disco in Charlotte. I remember driving for over 2 hours to Charlotte and 2 hours back home almost every Friday night. I needed to connect with people who behaved like me. I felt totally disconnected from my LGBT community. Later, I realized that there was another gay disco in Greensboro, where I used to live. It was the place where I met Chris (pseudonym), a bipolar white man, who visited Panama while dating me and changed me for another guy. This gay disco was also the place where I met Rob, the man who has been my partner and friend for over 23 years.

1   Origins

Over the years, I have been able to visit my homeland once or twice a year. I have reconnected with my old friends and made new friends. I have always liked to read and write. Both skills became my refuge ever since I was very

young. Reading allowed me to find the answers to questions that I was not per-
mitted to ask, and writing became the place for me to express my feelings, fears,
and identities. So every time I left Panama, I wondered about my gay friends'
situations. I always struggled to understand how homophobia was internalized
in their conversations. I struggled to understand how issues of class, language
(use of words in the English language), beauty (from a white Eurocentric lens),
and racism were embedded in my community. I realized that although my
friends wanted to let me know that things were better in the country in terms
of acceptance toward the LGBT community, I discovered that on a deeper
level, things were still the same or worse. My only way to deal with thoughts
about my peers' situations was through my writing. I used my trip back home
to write on the plane. I wrote some testimonials and poems. I saved them for a
while since I thought that no one really cared about this type of writing until
I started pursuing my doctoral studies at The University of North Carolina at
Greensboro. It was there that I met Professor Silvia Bettez, who later became
my mentor, colleague, and friend. Silvia created the space for me to talk about
my sexuality as a queer and immigrant man. It was Silvia who connected me
with other Latinx writers and scholars. It was in her courses that I discovered
that I was not alone, that my queer writings had a space in academia, and that
there were other *maricónes* in the United States who looked and wrote like me.

In 2015, I attended and presented the genesis of this study at the Association for Jotería Arts, Activism, and Scholarship (AJAAS) conference in Phoenix,
Arizona. I discovered a safe space where queer scholars and community activists voiced their personal and communal stories using a jotería epistemology.
Hames-Garcia (2014b) claims, "A jotería, our bodies and our selves are lived
legacies of colonialism, racism, xenophobia, homophobia, sexism, and hetero-
sexism" (p. 136). Within jotería studies, the political becomes personal meaning we cannot ignore our personal experiences while decolonizing traditional
epistemologies and advocating for social justice.

In 2017, I was able to publish *An Unhealed Wound: Growing up Gay in Panama*
(Ríos Vega, 2017a). It became my first published testimonial as a queer of color
scholar. I continued visiting my country and reconnecting with more folks. In
January 2018, I published my first Spanish book *Historias desde el Sexilio* (Stories
from the Sexile) which includes fictional stories where the characters discuss
some of the themes related to my community, such as homophobia, racism,
conversion therapy treatment, same-sex relationships, forbidden love, and religion. In addition, I have published my testimonials and about my transnational
mariposa consciousness epistemology in academic journals in Panama.

In June 2018, I decided to develop a large qualitative research study to
document the experiences of LGBT individuals in Panama. I realized that

there were no scholarly publications that documented my community. First, because talking about issues of sexuality, homophobia, and transphobia was not accepted in most academic spaces in the country. I could not find a single book that talked about Panama's LGBT population from a social justice standpoint. Rocha Cortez (2022) argues that "Our homosexual memories are silenced/subterranean discourses. We appear sketched and lightly named as picturesque or abject characters" (author's translation, p. 32).

One day, I said to myself that it was me who needed to start doing some academic research about this needed topic. I wanted others to read and hear my friends' testimonials. It became my goal to use my privilege as a translational researcher and *maricón* to document and publish my friends' experiences in academia. As an autoethnographer, I also wanted to include my own experiences as a transnational mariposa who crosses geographical borders to develop dual identities. In the United States, I claim to be a queer of color, while in Panama, I identify myself as a *maricón, cueco, pato,* and *loca.* Throughout these years as a transnational mariposa, I have joined LGBT organizations, attended conferences and panels, and participated in multiple events during Pride month in June. I have also interviewed and written papers in Spanish and English about the experiences of LGBT individuals in Panama. I am an active member of the Association of Joteria Studies and Arts (AJAAS), a Latinx queer academic organization in the United States. I have also joined a group of Central American gay writers and scholars, published some articles, and presented my studies online. All these spaces have allowed me to share and make visible the experiences of my community in Panama. I hope that this book will continue to allow readers to have a deeper and first-hand understanding of my journeys as a transnational mariposa (queer of color and *maricón*) and the lived experiences of LGBT individuals in Panama, which might or might not be very similar to the experiences of other LGBT individuals in Latin American countries.

As an educator and researcher in the Department of Education, Counseling, and Leadership in a predominantly White university in the Midwest of the United States, I found this book relevant within the field of education for various reasons. Having a different and fresh view of the experiences of LGBT communities in a Central American country will serve as a springboard to discuss how issues of diversity, sexuality, as well as homophobia and transphobia are experienced in other countries. This work will allow readers to have a deeper understanding of issues such as injustice, human rights, LGBT communities, and resilience experienced outside of the United States. Also, in my experience as a bilingual/international researcher, I have learned that English-speaking researchers have a hard time finding resources in English that document the experiences of LGBT communities in Latin American countries. Finally, this book will serve as an excellent source of information and advocacy to learn from those voices that have been silenced and ignored for many years.

It is through my constant trips to my homeland and my critical reflections about my self as a *maricón*/queer man that I can question the following:

- How can I use my transnational mariposa consciousness to document my lived experiences as a *maricón* in Panama?
- What does it mean to be a gay man in Panama nowadays?
- How do trans women's experiences with a hostile society shape their everyday existence?

2 Method

Drawing from queers of color epistemologies, jotería studies, and Daniel Enriquez Perez's (2014) mariposa consciousness, I developed a transnational mariposa consciousness as a Latin American man who self-identifies as a queer of color in the U.S., but through my constant trips to his homeland of Panama, my constant reflexivity pushes me to adopt a *maricón* identity to counteract oppression and invisibility. It is based on these geographical borders as a transnational that I share my personal experiences as an immigrant/Latino man of color that I make the political (queerness) something personal (*maricón*). It is important to understand that in order to develop my own transnational mariposa consciousness I need to know my own history and embrace all elements of my shifting identities. I understand that I cannot feel ashamed of who I am or of what I do naturally. Tijerilla Revilla and Santillana (2014) quote a jotería identity/consciousness:

1. Is rooted in fun, laughter, and radical queer love,
2. Is embedded in a Mexican, Latin American, Indigenous, and African diasporic past and present,
3. Is derived from the terms Jota and Joto and has been reclaimed as an identity/consciousness of empowerment,
4. Is based on queer Latina/o and Chicana/o and gender-nonconforming realities or lived experiences,
5. Is committed to multidimensional social justice and activism,
6. Values gender and sexual fluidity and expressions,
7. Values the exploration of identities individually and collectively,
8. Rejects homophobia, heteronormativity, racism, patriarchy, xenophobia, gender discrimination, classism, colonization, citizenism, and any other form of subordination,
9. Claims and is aligned with feminist/muxerista pedagogy and praxis
10. Claims an immigrant and working-class background/origin,

11.   Claims a queer Latina/o and Chicana/o ancestry, and
12.   Supports community members and family in their efforts to avoid and
        heal from multidimensional battle fatigue (pp. 174–175).

I use mariposa as a symbol of traveling, border crossings, critical lens, resiliency, and advocacy. Perez (2014) claims that many Chicano/a and Latino/a
artists and writers have used butterfly imagery to develop a mariposa consciousness as a decolonizing theory and as "a symbol of transformation, life,
death, resiliency, migration, and the soul" (p. 99). As a transnational mariposa,
I keep crossing territorial and social borders that sometimes leave me tired
and hopeless. This border-crossing makes me wonder about my own self and
whether someone can claim to be a queer of color in one space and *maricón* in
a different space. It is this transnational identity shifting that always reminds
me that I live in what Anzaldúa (2007) referred to as "borderlands, a vague
and undetermined place created by the emotional residue of an unnatural
boundary" (p. 25), making me realize that I belong to "los atravesados." It is
this transnational consciousness that allows me to develop my own mariposa consciousness. I am learning to be a queer of color in the U.S. but also
become consciously aware of my flesh and soul as *maricón* in Panama. As a
transnational mariposa, I experience oppression and discrimination for being
an immigrant of color in the U.S., and in Panama, I struggle with witnessing
how homophobia, transphobia, sexism, racism, classism, and other layers of
discrimination are understood by my own people as normal. I understand that
I must face homophobia and a double-standard society in Panama and a racist and xenophobic space in the U.S. Like Anzaldúa's (2007) *mestiza*, I have a
"struggle of borders, an inner war." Living in two different cultures and countries, I get different messages from people. In the U.S., I can be oppressed for
having a brown body and accented English; whereas, in Panama, I experience
oppression because of my mannerisms or for being labeled *maricón, cueco, and
loca* for my mannerisms and/or for never being married at my age.

As with Anzaldúa's (2007) *mestiza,* my transnational mariposa consciousness makes me more reflective about myself and my identity shifting. I take
this identity shifting as the constant transformation of my mariposa consciousness. It is during this transformation when I open my "alas" (wings) and
find liberation; it is through my writings, my testimonials, that I experience
resiliency. For Perez (2014),

> Having a mariposa consciousness is to recognize "our inner and outer
> beauty and strength; it is about being yourself in your true nature, in your
> own words, in all your mariposada—the full splendor of your beauty,
> strength, gender expression, and sexuality. It is about knowing your

history and yourself fully and embracing all aspects of your identity. It is about maintaining a physical and mental equilibrium so that you can soar in all your glory. (p. 102)

2.1 Autoethnographer's Data

To describe the above questions, I reflect on my own experience as a self-identified *maricón* in Panama. As an autoethnographer, I felt the need to document my lived experiences while still living in my home country. Although I reflected most of the time when I came back to the U.S. after visiting my mom and siblings, I always used my plane trips to document my concerns, pains, and sometimes anger about my LGBT community. I used to reconnect with my old friends to brainstorm about our experiences as maricónes, to compare how things used to be in the past, and to reflect on how much progress we have made as a community and society. After hearing my friends, I felt the urgency to document their voices as well. As an autoethnographer, I use my transnational mariposa consciousness to reflect on my own lived experiences as a *maricón* in Panama, I have been able to document my own anecdotes as a form of data in this qualitative study. Although I highlight my experience throughout most of this book, I also find similarities with other sources for insight, particularly interviews I developed with men who identified as gay and trans women.

2.2 Participants' Data

I started collecting data between 2018 and 2021 as part of a large qualitative research project. Most of the interviews were held face-to-face during my summer trips to Panama (Glense, 2006). I met with some old friends who agreed to be part of the study. First, we met at public cafe shops or restaurants. I talked to them about my study and the reason why it was important. Then we decided to schedule a day for the interview. I met most of the participants at a local library's reading room or a conference room in a hotel. I asked the participants to read and sign the consent forms. Once they signed the forms, I began asking my study's leading questions. I initiated our conversation with open-ended questions that allowed the participants to narrate personal anecdotes. During our conversation, I also shared some of my own personal experiences to make the interview process more engaging. Four of the participants agreed to be interviewed using the platform Whatsapp. In that case, I emailed the consent forms to the participants and asked them to read and sign them before they sent them back to me. Then we scheduled an online interview. Both interviews lasted between one and two hours.

The participants offered insightful information about what it means to be sexually diverse in Panama's society. Each participant was willing to share childhood, family, and school experiences while they developed their identities. Some of the narratives in this study, along with my own personal testimonials, corroborate the challenges of being self-identified in sexually diverse communities in a Latin American country. Some of the stories have left the participants with childhood scars, internalized homophobia, and mental health issues. Although the participants' narratives show that Panama is still an unsafe space for LGBT individuals, they also share how their *vulnerable bodies* learn to live and exist on the edges of a homophobic, transphobic, and double-standard society. It is important to highlight that as a bilingual researcher, I decided to keep the original version of my interviews. I did not want to appear as a translator of the participants' voices but as a linguistic bridge. I felt that it was important to keep the participants' comments in Spanish since some of the expressions were hard to translate. While doing the translations, I realized that some of them lose their historical, geographical, and cultural identities if they were translated into the English language. Finally, future and bilingual readers and researchers might want to read and analyze the data in its original language.

Using my personal reflections and the participants' experiences allowed me to find common patterns in the different narratives (Creswell & Poth, 2018; Glesne, 2006; Saldaña & Omasta, 2018). The participants' answers to my open-ended questions and my personal anecdotes served as the springboard to analyze the experiences of gay men and trans women in Panama. Also, my observations and constant reflections on Panama's social expectations regarding issues of gender and sexuality helped me to have a more in-depth critical social justice understanding of the LGBT communities in Panama. My active participation and collaboration during Pride Month gave me the opportunity to observe and share the same spaces with other LGBT individuals. Additionally, it allowed me to reflect on how things have or have not changed since I left Panama.

It is through my critical reflection as a transnational mariposa and bilingual autoethnographer, that I can disrupt norms of research practice and representation, work from insider knowledge, and maneuver pain, confusion, anger, and uncertainty to make life better for the LGBT community in Panama. Additionally, it is my intention that this book will allow the LGBT community in Panama to break the silence while voicing their experiences. Finally, it is my goal that this book will be accessible to all kinds of readers.

3   Summary

This study represents an urgent call to document the narratives of LGBT individuals from a Central American country and from a critical social justice perspective. As a queer of color academic and researcher living in the United States and visiting Panama at least twice a year, I find it a moral obligation to share my personal experiences as a self-identified gay man along with the narratives of other gay men in Panama. It is important to understand that there are almost no academic studies and no spaces that openly address and advocate for LGBT communities in Panama. Unfortunately, social media, mainstream society, religious groups, and even some politicians tend to perpetuate stereotypes and stigmas toward LGBT communities.

This book brings hope to a vulnerable and minoritized group that has been ignored and erased in mainstream academia for years. This book's goal is to echo the experiences of LGBT individuals, their childhood, family, school, and societal experiences while developing gay and trans identities in a homophobic and transphobic society. It also analyzes how the author and the participants learn to live with risk to their vulnerable bodies in a country that does not protect their human rights as LGBT.

4   Overview of the Chapters

The organization of this book is to trace what I call "voicing vulnerable bodies living on the edge" in Panama. Through my autoethnography as a transnational mariposa, I reflect on my personal experiences while still living in Panama and my yearly travels to my homeland. I connect my own personal experiences to the participants' testimonials. To document my participants, I use face-to-face and Whatsapp interviews and observations. It is through my constant reflection as a transnational mariposa that the participants and I discuss and analyze how to navigate and resist a homophobic and unsafe society. It is my goal that this book will allow LGBT individuals in Panama to become more visible and discussed in academic spaces, especially in departments of education. It is my hope that this study will fill the gap in academia with issues of gender, masculinity, and LGBT communities in Panama and the region.

Before delving into the empirical material, Chapter 1: "Living on the Edges" discusses the reason why I decided to develop my study. Drawing from Queers of Color epistemologies and a transnational mariposa consciousness, I explain how the use of a transnational mariposa consciousness as a theoretical framework and methodology leads the study. I also explain that the use of my personal experiences and the participants,' as forms of data collection, allowed me to develop the different themes in this book. Additionally, I include the leading questions used to develop my study. I will also review the literature about LGBT communities from previous authors in Panama. Finally, I include a summary of the book and how it will fill in the gap in literature while documenting my personal experiences and the participants' testimonials as LGBT individuals in Panama and the region, and its urgency in academia.

Chapter 2: "Being Born Different" talks about the participants' childhood experiences while feeling different from other boys and their realization of their interest in those of the same gender. The participants also share their personal anecdotes from being bullied at school to not fulfilling their roles as typical boys as well as how their male peers made fun of them, especially during physical education classes. Finally, I include how the participants challenged the use of the term "out of the closet" as they relate it to the U.S. American culture. Instead, they claim the term acceptance, as it is closer to Panama's social reality. In a funny manner, some of them joke about not having physical closets at their houses due to their level of poverty.

Chapter 3: "Having (Lack of) Support" discusses how the participants' parents' acceptance, or lack thereof, shaped their sexual orientation. In this chapter, the participants share how their parents rejected and sometimes physically punished them for being effeminate. Some of them talked about moving away from their parents' home to be more open about their sexuality. Others share how they hid their sexuality until they were older and became more independent. Finally, some of these gay men discuss how they had to confess their sexuality to their parents after being diagnosed HIV+. Finally, they talked about developing mental health issues due to the constant bullying and/or lack of support from their parents and peers.

Chapter 4: "Unpacking Homophobia" reveals the participants' insightful examples of internalized homophobia. Panama's colloquial language has many homophobic terms to refer to gay men, usually associated with being effeminate and weak. Unfortunately, due to a lack of a critical interpretation of this homophobic language, it is usually understood as something cultural or as the norm. When I asked the participants to share their experiences with externalized homophobia, it was very easy for them to relate it to song lyrics, the police department, religious leaders and politicians, and homophobic individuals, especially heterosexual men.

Chapter 5: "Facing Social Challenges" documents how the participants in this book faced discrimination from family and friends. Some others shared their observations of openly gay men being discriminated against at jobs for behaving too effeminately. Other participants claim that some gay men discriminate against other gay men for being too effeminate, in the lower class or not looking attractive enough. Others tend to perpetuate issues of heteronormativity with their gay partners while embracing an active (man) or passive (woman) role in their relationship. This chapter also discusses how individuals conform to a double standard society where openly gay men are socially accepted in specific spaces such as carnivals, beauty salons, and/or to decorate saint altars at Catholic churches but unwelcomed in strictly heterosexual spaces. This chapter analyzes the experiences of two participants who tested HIV+. Finally, it closes with some critical anecdotes about hate crime in LGBT communities and the fact that there is not a State law that typifies these types of crimes as hate crimes. Some gay men are killed by their partners, sex workers, and/or heterosexual men who like to have sex with men.

Chapter 6: "What about Trans?" analyzes the lived experiences of one of the most oppressed and marginalized dissident bodies in this study. Documenting the personal experiences of what it means to be a transvestite, transsexual, and transgender within Panama's society allows these voices to be heard and understood. The participants shared how they have been rejected and disowned by their own parents, and relatives and sometimes oppressed by other LGBT individuals and society. Others shared how they became victims of bullying and were made fun of at school by their peers and sometimes teachers, pushing them to abandon their education and leaving them no options but to end up working as hairdressers or sex workers.

Chapter 7: "A Hopeful Transnational Mariposa" answers the research questions that led this book. To answer these questions, I developed three subthemes: *Vulnerable Bodies*, *Gay Men Stereotypes*, *Trans Women's Journey*, and *Maricón Phobia*. I also analyze my implications on Queers of Color epistemologies and how my Transnational Mariposa Consciousness allowed me to create a space in academia to document the experiences of LGBT individuals in Panama. I conclude my book with *LGBT Rights Are Human Rights* to echo the importance of developing a critical understanding about LGBT bodies living in vulnerable edges.

Notes

1   Maricón, which translates as faggot, might be considered an offensive term depending on its context and content. The author uses maricón as a counteracting word of empowerment and defiance against a heteronormative society.
2   Offensive term to call gay men in Panama.
3   Offensive term to refer to gay men in many Latin American countries.

CHAPTER 2

Being Born Different

Los sentimientos que empecé a experimentar por él me asustaron
al principio. Un hombre, según había aprendido desde pequeño, no
tenía que sentir esas cosas por otro hombre.

BAÑOS, 2020, p. 177

The feelings I began to experience for him frightened me at first. A
man, as he had learned from childhood, did not have to feel these
things for another man.

∵

It was always the birthday parties, the dancing, the singing, and other artistic
performances that allowed me to be myself. I was living in my own world, and
I did not pay attention to the messages that I kept receiving from relatives and
friends. As a child, I thought that what I was doing was normal. I was shaking
my hips, performing, and talking like the Latina divas on television, to name a
few. I thought I was making people laugh without realizing that I was defining
a *maricón*. I did not realize that I was different from other boys until I reached
puberty. I dated some girls during middle and high school, probably to please
my mother who always questioned my sexuality, or my older brother who dis-
liked my sissiness; however, I used to have weekly sexual encounters with one
of my neighbors during my teenage years, but he was not understood as being
gay. While I developed affection for him, he never associated these encounters
with being gay. Most of the boys that I had sexual encounters with took it as
a sexual game or part of their boy explorations with sexuality. Some of those
boys attended the same middle and high school, but we never talked to each
other at school. I felt that they were embarrassed or ashamed after they had
been with me. I guessed that it was due to my effeminate mannerisms. I was
probably seen as the *maricón* and as opposed to them. Most of these boys got
married and have their own families now. It has been a while since I saw them
last. I left my mother's house when I was seventeen to pursue college in the city
of Panama and never returned to live there.

1   Childhood

Like me, all the participants in this study share how they started feeling different from other boys during their childhood. Many expressed how they never
noticed that what they were doing was wrong until other boys started calling
them homophobic slurs. I met Rodolfo through another friend of mine. We
had lunch and talked about many issues related to the LGBT community in
Panama. Rodolfo was 47 when I met him first. He was once part of the first
LGBT organization in Panama and was currently working in an HIV non-profit
organization. After that first meeting, I invited him to join my study and he
agreed. During the formal interviews, I asked all the participants to share when
they realized that they were different from other boys. I wanted to find some
commonalities in our stories. Rodolfo commented:

> Desde pequeñito 9 o 10 años yo sabía que me gustaban los niños y no las
> niñas. No voy a decir que algo estaba mal en mi porque nunca he pensado
> que algo estaba mal en mí, sino que me di cuenta que me gustaban los
> niños. Obviamente viniendo de una familia conservadora ultra católica no
> lo demostré hasta que vine a la ciudad de Panamá y aún así hasta viviendo
> acá en Panamá seguía viviendo en un mundo hetero normativo. Desde los
> 10 a los 18 viví mi vida. No quiero usar la palabra normal, viví como un niño
> heterosexual, pero sabiendo que me gustaban los chicos y no las chicas y
> no fue hasta los 24 años que tuve mi primera experiencia sexual.

> Since I was little, 9 or 10 years old, I knew that I liked boys and not girls.
> I will not say that something was wrong with me because I have never
> thought that something was wrong with me, but I realized that I liked
> boys. Obviously coming from an ultra-Catholic conservative family, I
> didn't show it until I came to Panama City and even so, even living here
> in Panama, I continued to live in a hetero-normative world. From age
> 10 to 18 I lived my life. I do not want to use the word normal, I lived as a
> heterosexual child, but knowing that I liked boys and not girls and it was
> not until I was 24 that I had my first sexual experience.

Rodolfo grew up in a rural town outside of Panama City until he moved to continue his elementary education and graduated from college with a bachelor's
degree in international affairs; however, due to Panama's lack of opportunities
and politics, he could not find a job in the government to execute his profession. While living with his parents, he did not notice that his mannerisms made
him different from other boys until he was bullied by other boys, which I will

address later in this chapter. It is important to mention that Rodolfo shared
with me how he was once caught kissing another boy when he was still living
with his parents. He said,

> Me gustaba un vecino de mi edad, me gustaba mucho. Ocurrió algo muy
> curioso. Esto nunca se lo he contado a nadie. Yo le llegué a dar un piquito
> al niño y la mamá nos vio, pero nunca dijo nada. Era un niño muy lindo.
> El papá era chiricano y ella era del pueblo. Era mucho más blanco que
> yo, tenía los ojos como decimos aquí en Panamá, rayados. Era un niño
> guapísimo, me gustaba mucho.

> I liked a little neighbor my age, I liked him a lot. Something very curious
> happened. I have never told anyone about this. I got to give the child a
> kiss and his mother saw us, but she never said anything. He was a very
> cute child. The father was Chiricano and the mom was from there in the
> town. He was much whiter than me. His eyes, as we say here in Panama,
> hazel. He was a very handsome boy. I liked him a lot.

Similarly, Bolívar, a 48 year old civil engineer, grew up in the countryside
during his childhood where social and gender expectations are stricter and
usually based on religious beliefs. Bolivar came from a middle-class family,
which makes a huge difference, especially when you are "maricón." Again, Like
Rodolfo, Bolivar was not aware that his effeminate behavior made him different from other boys until he started attending school. He mentioned,

> Cuando entré a la escuela, los niños, principalmente los mayores que yo,
> me llamaron la atención de que había algo muy diferente en mi. Me decían
> cueco, cuequito, mariconcito, que yo no sabía ni qué significaban. Pero un
> recuerdo que sí tengo muy vivido. Es de niño que a ellos les interesaba o les
> llamara tanto la atención si yo movía mucho las manos, como yo hablaba,
> o como yo me manejaba. Luego un par de años después en la escuela, yo si
> me di cuenta rápidamente que yo era diferente a mis amiguitos.

> When I entered school, the children, mainly those older than me, called
> to attention that there was something very different about me. They
> called me cueco, cuequito, mariconcito, and I didn't even know what they
> meant. But I have a very vivid memory in my mind. It is as a child that
> they were interested or would call so much attention if I moved my hands
> a lot, how I spoke, or how I handled myself. Then a couple of years later in
> school, I quickly realized that I was different from my friends.

Bolivar mentioned how other boys made him feel different. They reminded him that there was something wrong with his sexuality. Bolivar understood that he was different, but he did not understand what it was. When he reached puberty he realized that he started to feel physical and sexual attraction for boys instead of girls. He said how he never talked to anybody about it since almost no one in his family talked about these issues. Homosexuality was seen as a sinful act.

Like Rodolfo and Bolivar, Juan, who was 33 years old and attending the University of Panama when I interviewed him, grew up in the countryside of Panama. I met Juan when he was a volunteer for a non-profit organization. He and I agreed to meet after I met him at a local cultural event at the French Cultural Center in downtown Panama. Interestingly, during the interview, Juan shared an anecdote about his feelings for one of his friends when he was in second grade. He said,

> Yo tenía un amiguito de segundo grado. Yo era sobrino de una de las maestras y él era sobrino de otra maestra. Mi tía me llevaba al colegio y pasaba por él a buscarlo. No, a él lo llevaban y nosotros lo llevamos de regreso a su casa. Recuerdo mis sentimientos de tristeza cuando él se bajaba del carro. Yo jugaba con él y lo recuerdo con mucha ilusión. Nunca más lo vi. Siento que esa fue mi primera ilusión de niño. Una vez me recuerdo haber llorado porque él se bajaba del carro. Fue algo muy extraño. Yo tenía 8 años. Él estaba en segundo y yo estaba en tercer grado.

> I had a friend in second grade. I was the nephew of one of the teachers and he was the nephew of another teacher. My aunt took me to school and stopped by to pick him up. His parents took him to school and we took him back to his house. I remember my feelings of sadness when he got out of the car. I played with him and I remember him with great enthusiasm. I never saw him again. I feel like that was my first excitement as a boy. Once I remember crying because he got out of the car. It was very strange. I was 8 years old. He was in second grade and I was in third grade.

Oscar, a high school teacher, was 34 when I interviewed him. We became friends after I gave a presentation at the annual English teachers' conference. After my talk, he approached me. I immediately realized that Oscar was gay after I asked if the guy who was with him was his boyfriend (Enrique). Of course, he was. Since then, Oscar and Enrique have been friends every time I visit Panama. When I asked him about his experiences with being different from other boys, his comments were very different from Bolivar, Juan, and Rodolfo. Oscar received homophobic slurs from his classmates from elementary school and even in college since it took him a long time to accept his sexual orientation. He expressed,

Bueno mi infancia fue bastante normal hasta los 10 años porque fue allí que noté que mis compañeros de clase se burlaban; lo que hoy se llama bullying. En ese tiempo no se llamaba de esa manera. Yo no entendía porque se burlaban. No entendía porque me decían que era maricón o que era cueco. La palabra que usan acá mucho, palabra despectiva que hiere bastante. Cada vez que me decían así, me iba para la casa confundido. Eso fue creando confusión en cuanto a mi identidad hasta los 23 años, incluso a nivel universitario el bullying continuó y fue aún peor. Como te dije, desde los diez 10 años me he sentido diferente a los demás niños. Todo era como una mezcla. Tuve mi primera relación con otro chico a los 28 años.

Well, my childhood was quite normal until I was 10 years old because it was there that I noticed my classmates making fun; what they call bullying today. At that time, it was not called this. I did not understand why they were teasing. I didn't understand why they told me I was a "maricón" or that I was a "cueco." The word they use here a lot, a derogatory word that hurts a lot. Every time they called me this, I would go home confused. That was creating confusion regarding my identity until I was 23 years old, even at the university level the bullying continued and was even worse. As I mentioned, since I was 10 years old I have felt different from other children. Everything was like a mix. I had my first relationship with another boy at 28 years old.

One of the most salient comments that these participants have in common is that although they realized that they were different from other boys, they felt that it was "normal" until they started getting homophobic remarks and/or physical violence at school for being effeminate. Others who realized that it was not socially acceptable that a boy would like another boy, preferred to keep it as a secret until they moved away from home. Adams (2021) explains how once a gay man comes out to his family, familial love and support sometimes become conditional and/or disappear. I also experienced the same phase. It was not until I left my mother's house in the countryside, when I experienced some form of "liberación sexual." It was through a dance class on Saturdays that I met other gay men in the city like I mentioned at the beginning of this book. Although I developed some attractions for some of my male college friends, I never mentioned anything about sexuality since I was afraid to be rejected. Being from the countryside put me in a vulnerable situation since there is a stigma that countryside people speak Spanish with a different accent, which is associated with being unintelligent or ignorant sometimes.

Being oppressed for speaking Spanish with a different accent was enough for me, so talking openly about my sexuality had no room.

2   School Bullying

> Boys changed clothes in front of everybody. They played jokes, pulled their pants down. I used to laugh like everybody else, but I was even more excited to see them all naked. I used to love it. (Enrique)

Being in school made gay individuals become vulnerable to being rejected, bullied, and even experienced physical violence. I was called all kinds of names when I was in school since I never defined what a boy was supposed to be or to perform like. I loved poetry, dancing, baking, and cooking, and was always around girls. I was never good at sports. I had terrible experiences playing soccer and basketball. The only game that I liked the most was baseball since boys and girls played in my neighborhood. Besides being an elementary school teacher, my mother was also a dressmaker. So I learned how to use her sewing machine. I loved sewing dresses for my neighbors' dolls. I enjoyed making piñatas and playing girls' games. All these girl-only performances made me extremely happy but also vulnerable to being called homophobic slurs and insults even by my older brother. It was a girly performance that made me the target of older boys and men who eventually sexually harassed me or made fun of me.

As I introduced in the previous section, it was the school where most of the participants experienced being questioned for being too effeminate or hanging out with girls. Additionally, sports also have been taught to be gendered (boys/girls) spaces. Unfortunately, since early boys are reminded that they need to play with other boys and girls need to play with girls, physical education classes, contests, folk dance groups, and other social events are still gendered boys and girls. The minute one gender crosses that social expectation, that individual's sexuality is scrutinized and questioned. Children start getting this gender expectation reminder early in their lives. A lot of them, like me, experience being bullied by their own parents and relatives without knowing it, creating all kinds of insecurities and low self-esteem. Felipe, a 24-year-old college student, talked to us about how he experienced being bullied for hanging out with girls. He said,

> De niño me decían mariconcito un compañero de escuela porque siempre estaba jugando con las niñas, ya que jugar con las niñas todo el tiempo es sinónimo de que tu eres gay aquí en Panamá, por lo menos en mi época.

When I was a child, my classmate used to call me "mariconcito" since I was always playing with the girls. Playing with girls all the time is synonymous with being gay here in Panama, at least during my childhood.

Felipe mentioned how bad he was at sports. One of the biggest challenges that teenage boys face while playing sports, which is a form of socialization, takes place when they test each other's masculinity, and how strong and good at sports they are. This is a constant competition to show off who is stronger and better and when a boy does not follow those social expectations, his sexuality is questioned. Like Felipe, I was never good at sports. I was always afraid of being hurt or outed by my peers since I was not good at any sport. I was always worried about being called "maricón" for not knowing how to play. Although I liked boys, I was always afraid to be around them when they were in groups since they were constantly bullying and making fun of each other. I was scared to be bullied in public for not being "macho" enough.

Juan, Oscar, Rodolfo, and Enrique (Oscar's boyfriend) shared how they received discrimination during physical education classes for not playing with other boys. Instead, they were bullied as "maricones" or "cuecos." Juan mentioned,

> Yo creo que fui un niño afeminado. Recuerdo que en el colegio jugaba con las niñas béisbol y los niños jugaban fútbol. Yo jugaba béisbol y siempre había esa pregunta por parte de los niños de que porque tu no juegas con nosotros. Eso fue como en cuarto, quinto y sexto grado. En primaria se burlaban de mí porque jugaba con las niñas. Me decían pato, cueco. Me gustaba jugar más béisbol que fútbol.

> I think I was an effeminate child. I remember that in school I played baseball with the girls and the boys played soccer. I played baseball and there was always that question from the children, "Why don't you play with us?" That was like fourth, fifth, and sixth grade. In elementary school, they made fun of me because I played with the girls. They called me "pato" and "cueco." I liked to play more baseball than soccer.

Similarly, Oscar commented,

> En la escuela me acuerdo en quinto grado, mis compañeros, especialmente cuando estábamos en educación física o en agricultura. A mí no me gustaba el fútbol. A mí me gustaba el voleibol, pero entonces era amanerado cuando jugaba. De ahí empezó ese bullying contra mí. Me decían todo tipo de cosas. Después llegaba a la casa y no quería comer después

de tantos insultos. Al día siguiente iba con miedo de entrar al salón. Primero que no entendía qué estaba pasando. Esa era mi duda más grande. Yo no entendía qué estaba pasando con esa parte del maltrato de mis compañeros de clase. Bueno eso me pasó en secundaria donde sí recibí abuso por parte de mis compañeros. Me pegaron, gritando cosas, y hasta me pegaron por mi forma de ser. Fueron patadas. Me pegaron puños en la cara. Me dijeron, "maricón, hasta cuando vas a dejar de ser maricón."

In school, I remember in fifth grade, my classmates, especially when we were in physical education or agriculture. I did not like soccer. I liked volleyball, but then I was very effeminate when I played. That's where that bullying against me started. They said all kinds of things to me. Later I would come home and did not want to eat after so many insults. The next day I was afraid to enter the room. First, I did not understand what was happening. That was my biggest doubt. I did not understand what was happening with that other than the mistreatment of my classmates. Well, that happened to me in high school where I did receive abuse from my classmates. They hit me, they shouted things and they even hit me for how I was. They kicked me. They beat me in my face. They said, "Maricón, when are you going to stop being maricón."

Like Juan and Oscar, Rodolfo shared,

En mi infancia no, pero en mi adolescencia si en primer ciclo. Yo detesto los deportes. En Panamá hay una materia que es educación física y meterme a jugar fútbol y sentirme todo sudado me daba asco. Yo siempre llevaba una excusa médica. Entonces los compañeros me empezaron a hacer bullying porque no quería jugar fútbol ni baloncesto. Ellos decían que era maricón por eso. Tenía un amigo, lo considero amigo porque aún hablamos, me dijo que lo curioso es que yo era siempre el primero en las duchas. Es que cuando decían vayan a bañarse yo siempre era el primero porque en mi salón había un chino panameño que me gustaba y ellos empezaron a darse cuenta y me hacían burlas de que yo era maricón, que yo era cueco, que me gustaban los hombres. Nunca llegaron a violencia física. Yo le digo a mis amigos que el acoso verbal también es malo, puede ser mas malo aun que el acoso físico porque si la persona no está emocionalmente preparada puede llevarlo a quitarse la vida.

Not in my childhood, but in my adolescence, yes, during middle school. I hate sports. In Panama there is a subject that is physical education and playing soccer and feeling all sweaty made me sick. I always carried a medical excuse. Then my classmates started bullying me because I didn't want to play soccer or basketball. They said I was a "maricón" for that. I had a friend, I consider him a friend because we still talk, he told me that the funny thing is that I was always the first in the showers. It is that when they said go to bathe I was always the first because in my classroom there was a Panamanian Chinese that I liked and they began to realize and made fun of me that I was a "maricón," that I was a "cueco," that I liked men. They never amounted to physical violence. I tell my friends that verbal harassment is also bad, it can be even worse than physical harassment because if the person is not emotionally prepared it can lead to suicide.

Enrique mentioned,

Bueno algunas veces me rechazaban para algunas actividades, físicas más que todo, y en educación física. Cuando iba a jugar fútbol, se burlaban de mí por mi forma de correr. En una ocasión participé en un partido de fútbol de niños y niñas. Yo casi nunca había jugado fútbol, pero en esta ocasión me pusieron a jugar. Y bueno, algunas veces gritaba. Al final del partido mis compañeros me reclamaron que yo estaba gritando como mujer.

Well sometimes I was rejected for some activities, physical more than anything, and in physical education. When I went to play soccer, they made fun of me for my running. I once participated in a boys and girls soccer game. I had hardly ever played soccer, but this time they pushed me to play. Well, sometimes I would scream. At the end of the game my teammates claimed that I was screaming like a woman.

During the interviews, other participants shared how they suffered from bullying and sometimes physical violence for being effeminate or doing things that were only socially accepted in boys. Like any other Latin American and conservative society, Panama's gender expectations are clearly defined by tough sports and boys hanging out with boys. Once a boy breaks those social norms, his sexuality is questioned. Unfortunately, a lot of boys do not report those incidents since it is expected that boys take care of their own problems or some of them do not want to be understood as weak and/or girlish while accusing their oppressors. Julio, who was always an effeminate boy, shared how he was beaten up by his peers while in elementary school. He shared,

Cuando estaba en segundo grado, 20 niños de mi salón de clase me agarraron a patadas en el baño de la escuela sin que la directora hiciera absolutamente nada. Nadie hizo absolutamente nada. Los niños me gritaban, "chiquillo maricón, quiere seguir siendo gay? Quiere seguir siendo amanerado? Tienes que ser hombre." Me agarraban, me pateaban. Eso sucedió durante el recreo. La única que hizo algo fue mi mamá que trabajaba en la escuela y la maestra, quien mandó a citar a los padres, pero los padres como siempre defendiendo a sus hijos.

When I was in second grade, 20 boys from my classroom kicked me in the school bathroom with the principal doing absolutely nothing. Nobody did anything at all. The boys yelled at me, "You maricón boy, do you want to stay gay? Do you want to remain effeminate? You have to be a man." They grabbed and kicked me. That happened during recess. The only one who did something was my mother who worked at the school as a teacher, who sent for the parents, but the parents, as always, defended their children.

Like Enrique's story with issues of bullying and physical violence, Anibal, a 58-year-old librarian and LGBT activist, who from his childhood fell in love with ballet, received constant homophobic slurs and insults for doing something that is usually assigned to girls. He commented how when his mother took him to register for his first ballet lessons, the secretary of the National School of Dance looked at him in a suspicious manner for being a boy. He shared how dancing ballet became his way to express himself since he knew that society did not accept him for being an effeminate boy. He mentioned,

Estudié ballet desde los 8 años hasta los 19. Pero yo tenía que enfrentar al machismo de la sociedad cuando a veces hacíamos presentaciones en eventos públicos. Cuando la gente veía a un niño de 8, 9, 10 años bailando con todas estas niñas, ellos me gritaban barbaridades. Se reían de mí. Me gritaban marica. Yo haciendo lo que me que me encantaba y tener que soportar las burlas de la gente era algo bien traumático para mí. Eso me daba mucha rabia.

I studied ballet from the age of 8 to 19. But I had to face the machismo of society when we sometimes made presentations at public events. When people saw an 8, 9, 10-year-old boy dancing with all these girls, they yelled a lot at me. They laughed at me. They called me queer. Doing what I loved and having to endure the ridicule of people was very traumatic for me. That made me very angry.

También en la escuela fui objeto de bullying porque mucha gente me veía en televisión bailando. En el vecindario también recibí bullying. En el vecindario me gritaban cueco, maricón. Ese tipo de cosas. Pero yo te puedo decir que yo fui violado dos veces porque eso me exponía. La primera vez por poco me matan. Yo tendría como 10, 11 años y los muchachos eran como de 15, 16 años. Después de que hicieron lo que les dio la gana conmigo me dieron una golpiza terrible que casi quedé inconsciente.

I was also bullied at school because many people saw me dancing on television. In the neighborhood I was also bullied. In the neighborhood they called me cueco, faggot. That kind of thing. But I can tell you that I was raped twice because it exposed me. The first time they almost killed me. I was like 10, 11 years old and the boys were like 15, 16 years old. After they did what they wanted with me, they gave me a terrible beating that almost made me unconscious.

Recuerdo que cuando salía de la Escuela Belisario Porras, iba a las prácticas de ballet en la academia de danza y a veces mis compañeros me sacaban las mallas y los zapatos y se las ponían para burlarse de mí. Una vez la directora de la escuela me tuvo como de dos o tres horas parado al sol, en el patio de la escuela, parado como un soldado porque según ella yo había fomentado cosas indebidas en el salón de clase. Tu te imaginas ver toda la escuela, todo mundo asomado por la ventana viendo lo que estaba pasando y yo parado allí. Yo no me podía mover. En ese tiempo tenía como 9 o 10 años.

I remember that when I was leaving the Belisario Porras School, I would go to ballet practices at the dance academy and sometimes my classmates would take off my tights and shoes and put them on to make fun of me. Once the school principal kept me standing in the sun for about two or three hours, in the schoolyard, standing like a soldier because according to her I had encouraged inappropriate things in the classroom. You imagine seeing the whole school, everyone leaning out the window seeing what was happening and me standing there. I couldn't move. At that time, I was about 9 or 10 years old.

Cristobal, a 29-year-old medical doctor, who grew up in the countryside, talked about how he never denied his sexual orientation and how it led him to experience bullying in school and his neighborhood. He had no choice but to learn to fight to be himself. He mentioned,

Desde niño sufrí mucho de acoso. Esas peleas son las que te definen. A mi me llegaron a golpear varias veces, no por ser afeminado o partido sino

porque nunca negué que me gustaban los varones. Sufrí golpes, humilla-
ciones públicas en el parque. En primaria recibí ataques. Después en la
secundaria fue incrementando al punto que yo comencé a defenderme
ya de vuelta. Eso me costó un par de expulsiones ya que las sanciones
iban hacia mi no a los que me agredían. Yo no era el unico homosexual
en la escuela. Había unos más afeminados y con ellos también se metían.

Since I was a child, I suffered a lot from bullying. Those fights are what
define you. They hit me several times, not because I was effeminate or
openly gay, but because I never denied that I liked men. I suffered blows,
public humiliations in the park. In elementary school I received attacks.
Later in high school, it increased to the point that I began to defend
myself right back. That cost me a couple of expulsions since the sanc-
tions went to me, not to those who attacked me. I was not the only homosexual in school. There were some more effeminate and with them, there
was also bullying.

It is clear to conclude that all of us suffered gender discrimination, bullying,
and physical violence in sports due to our sexuality or lack of a male "macho"
performance. It is on the field where boys start questioning their peers' sexuality. Some of the participants shared how they were called names for not
doing what boys were supposed to do when on the field. Some others tried to
perform their very best to please social expectations, but it was still not good
enough to prevent their peers from calling them "cuecos" or "maricónes" and
to be reminded about their sexuality. The saddening part about these experiences is that there was a lack of adult supervision at school to prevent these
incidents from taking place and a lack of sexuality education that would allow
students in general to critically analyze gender as a social construct. All the
participants, including myself, still struggle to reflect on these incidents with
bullying for not being able to be masculine enough for our peers. We all agree
that it is the schools' and teachers' responsibility to protect all students, especially those who are part of the LGBT community since they are usually very
vulnerable to their male peers.

3   Acceptance

I remember that I always liked to dance for as long as I can recall. I danced
to Menudo songs with my friends in my neighborhood. At school, I was cho-
sen to dance at homecoming celebrations and school anniversaries. While in

middle school, I won a poetry contest and represented the school, competing with other students in the district. I did not win the district contest but became very famous at my school. I met new friends after that, but some other classmates started calling me names, which I did not pay much attention to. During my childhood and early adolescence, I had no idea how all these things that I enjoyed doing were related to issues of gender expectations, especially for girls instead of boys. Occasionally, my older brother reminded me that I was doing girls' things, but I never paid attention to him since we never got along. Later, I got the same homophobic remarks from classmates and some neighbors. This may be the reason why it is hard for me to accept being a *maricón*. I was happy being myself, the dancer, the poet, or the cook, and never associated it with a female role. It was society that reminded me that what I was doing was not acceptable. I learned to create my own world. I learned to love reading books and to start planning my own destiny. After I finished high school, I realized that I was different from other boys. I could not stand my brother's homophobic reminders of my sexuality. I wanted to pursue higher education away from my relatives. Pantoja Guzmán (2021) argues, "There is blatant discrimination towards people who don't fit into the established molds" (p. 130). According to him, we (gay men) have no choice but to behave based on "established norms." When the opportunity arrived, I packed my suitcase and left my mom's house. I moved away from home, but I lived with some relatives for 3 years in the city. I had no choice but to hide my sexuality. I was a full-time student with no job and money, so I had to keep my secret of being queer while living with relatives.

When I asked the participants about the expression "Step out of the closet," most of them refused to use that term. Some of them suggested using the term "acceptance" instead. Others argued that stepping out of the closet assumes that the individual has been hiding from others or that closets are spaces to hang clothes not people. Esteban, a 54-year-old businessman, for example, claimed that it is a white American term that cannot be applied to Panama. He suggested that the moment an individual becomes aware of his/her/their sexual orientation, it is considered a form of acceptance. He added that some people do not accept their sexuality due to fear, while others prefer to live a double life. "They live an unhappy life when they do not accept themselves." He mentioned,

> Yo me acepté como a los 10, 11 años pero tuve una vida bisexual hasta los 29 años. Tenía relación con hombres y mujeres. Tengo un hijo. Viví con una mujer por 7 años. Después tuve otra relación con otra chica que duró como tres años. Siempre entraba con mi verdad en la mano. Les decía que también me acostaba con hombres. La mamá de mi hijo me conoció desde la universidad y siempre supo. Todas las mujeres que tuve en vida sabían de

antemano mi otra cara. De aceptar que tenía más gusto hacia los hombres fue como a los 11 años. Pero aun así seguí teniendo relaciones con hombres y con mujeres. La última relación que tuve con una mujer fue a los 30.

I accepted myself when I was 10, 11 years old but I had a bisexual life until I was 29 years old. I had relationships with men and women. I have a son. I lived with a woman for 7 years. Then I had another relationship with another girl that lasted like three years. I always came in with my truth in hand. I told them that I also slept with men. My son's mother has known me since college and always knew. All the women I had in life knew beforehand my other side. Acceptance that I had more taste towards men came around 11 years old. But even so, I continued to have relationships with men and women. The last relationship I had with a woman was at 30.

Like Esteban, Raúl, Antonio, Julio, Rodolfo, and Oscar agreed that the term acceptance should be used instead of "to step out of the closet." Some of them see it as an obsolete and North American term that does not apply to Panama's reality. Others defined "the closet" as a physical space used to store or hide things, while still others defined "the closet" as a place to hide from society or to deny an individual's real self. It is important to highlight that Esteban, like me, came from a different generation when the term "out of the closet" was not part of our language. I am not surprised, like many other sexual identities and gender expressions, that the term "out of the closet" is another example of social media influence as part of our capitalistic world. I met Raúl, a 51-year-old Afro-Panamanian man, while I was still living in Panama. I used to visit gay clubs on weekends where he used to impersonate famous Latina divas like La Lupe, Edita Nazario, and Amanda Miguel, to mention a few. Raúl became and still is an iconic figure in the gay community of Panama. Whenever I go to Panama, I find out where he is having his show, so I can visit him. Being able to see Raúl on stage after twenty years living in the United States, also allows me to reflect on how many things have or have not changed since I left Panama. When I asked Raúl about the expression "out of the closet," he mentioned,

Nosotros no somos muda de ropa. Que yo sepa nunca he salido de ningún closet. Yo nunca he vivido dentro de un armario. Para mí un clóset es lo que tú no quieres ver a simple vista. En un closet está la ropa, están los zapatos viejos y está la correa. Una cosa que no quieres que nadie vea, lo tuyo íntimo. Entonces yo no creo que estas cosas tengan que estar guardadas. Ese término no me gusta este término prefiero mejor te descubriste o te aceptaste, porque a veces el problema no es el miedo a que te acepten sino el aceptarse uno primero.

We are not changing clothes. To my knowledge I have never come out of any closet. I have never lived in a closet. For me, a closet is what you don't want to see with the naked eye. In a closet are the clothes, there are the old shoes and there is the belt. One thing you do not want anyone to see, your intimacy. So I don't think these things have to be guarded. I don't like this term, the term I prefer is that you better discover or accept yourself, because sometimes the problem is not the fear of being accepted but accepting yourself first.

He argued that "to step out of closet" is a term that LGBT individuals have taken from the English language and that does not translate to Panama's reality. During our conversations, I also learned that Raúl's mother and relatives have never questioned his sexuality, instead they have always accepted him. Raúl is a very talented man, who has always openly talked about his sexuality on TV and expressed it during carnival, which is one of the most famous cultural events in Panama. Besides being an impersonator, he is also a custom designer, especially for carnival queens.

Antonio, a 52-year-old theater director and actor, added,

Salir del clóset es decirle al mundo que eres lo que eres, no creo que así sea la cosa. Yo creo que todo debe estar en su lugar. Yo digo que cada quien tiene su vida. Yo digo que salí del closet a los 26 años cuando decidí tener pareja. Yo digo que salir del clóset es aceptarse a sí mismo.

Coming out of the closet is telling the world that you are what you are, I don't think that's the way it is. I think everything should be in its place. I say that everyone has their own life. I say that I came out of the closet at 26 when I decided to have a partner. I say coming out is accepting yourself.

Julio, a 19-year-old and unemployed, commented that LGBT individuals do not live in a closet since society is the biggest closet, where people have no choice but to hide who they really are. He argued,

Siento que el armario no existe. El armario está hecho para la ropa, no para las personas. Cuando se usa esa expresión salir del armario es prácticamente para decir que se sienten reprimidos en un lugar en específico, pero no en un armario. En un armario que nos mantiene encerrado, que nos pone claustrofóbicos y este lugar se refleja en la sociedad. La sociedad en específico es nuestro armario. Es ese grupo de personas que forman unas cuatro paredes que por su repudio, su odio, nos hacen sentir que estamos encerrados en un lugar. Pero la verdad creo que está un poco mal dirigida. La expresión salir del armario, simplemente no nos permiten ser libres. No creo que sea recomendable usar ese término porque el armario es para la ropa. Vamos a decir tengo miedo de salir a la sociedad y al fin voy a salir y ser quien soy. Usar las palabras textuales correctas para nosotros, sentirnos orgullosos de decir soy gay, soy homosexual, ser esto, ser lo otro pero me siento orgulloso.

I feel like the closet doesn't exist. The closet is made for clothes, not for people. When that expression is used to come out of the closet it is practically saying that they feel repressed in a specific place, but not in a closet. In a closet that keeps us locked up, that makes us claustrophobic, and this place is reflected in society. Society specifically is our closet. It is that group of people that form our four walls that by their repudiation, their hatred, make us feel that we are locked in a place. But the truth is, I think it is a little misdirected. The expression coming out of the closet just doesn't allow us to be free. I do not think it is advisable to use that term because the closet is for clothes. We are going to say I am afraid to go out into society and at last, I am going to go out and be who I am. Use the correct textual words for us, be proud to say I am gay, I am homosexual, be this, be that, but I am proud.

Similarly, Rodolfo agreed,

Yo creo que no, siento que a veces nos auto sumergimos en eso del armario, pero yo creo que tanto las etiquetas como el armario son para la ropa no para las personas. Creo que inconscientemente por querer protegernos, por querer que no nos hieran, que no nos lastimen, nos metemos en ese armario imaginario, pero no estoy muy de acuerdo con esa expresión. Existen personas que usan esa jerga de estás en el armario o salir del closet porque viven una doble vida y no los critico porque es su forma de autoprotegerse, tanto hombres como mujeres para que no los lastimen.

I don't think—I feel that sometimes we submerge ourselves in that closet, but I believe that both the labels and the closets are for clothes not for people. I think that unconsciously by wanting to protect ourselves, by wanting them not to hurt us, to not to be hurt, we get into that imaginary closet, but I don't quite agree with that expression. There are people who use that jargon of you are in the closet or coming out of the closet because they live a double life and I do not criticize them because it is their way of protecting themselves, both men and women, so that they do not get hurt.

Oscar analyzed the expression "to step out of the closet" as a process where individuals get to accept themselves to be happy. He shared,

> Para mí salir del closet es un proceso. Creo que la frase salir del clóset es una frase muy espontánea. Pienso que no se acerca a lo que realmente uno vive. Pienso que salir del clóset eso va poco a poco. Es un proceso. Primero uno tiene que aceptarse uno mismo, salir de la cárcel que tiene uno por dentro. Yo ya salí de la cárcel porque antes tenía miedo, estrés. Cuando iba caminando la gente se burlaba de mí, como los años anteriores cuando estaba en la secundaria y en la primaria. Ahora no me importa. Ahora soy yo. Ahora me siento mejor conmigo mismo. Me estoy sintiendo libre. Todavía faltan ciertas barreras que debo derribar, pero sé que lo voy a hacer.

> Coming out of the closet is a process for me. I think the phrase coming out of the closet is a very spontaneous phrase. I think that it is not close to what one really lives. I think coming out of the closet takes place little by little. It is a process. First one must accept oneself, get out of the prison that one has inside. I already got out of jail because before I was afraid and stressed. When I was walking, people made fun of me, like the previous years when I was in middle school and elementary school. Now I don't care. Now I am me. Now I feel better about myself. I am feeling free. There are still certain barriers that I must break down, but I know I will.

Carlos Decena (2011) in his book *Tacit Subjects*, argues that the men that he interviewed for his book understood their sexuality as something "present" instead of something that must be reminded by society. He added, "Some queers of color have an uneasy relationship with the closet because they resist the depoliticized 'liberation' that coming out promises, which currently resides in a gay identity as a sociocultural formation and as a niche market" (pp. 18–19).

I feel that there must be a distinction between accepting yourself as a queer individual and talking about it in public spaces, which to me is very risky since it places the individual in an extremely vulnerable position. Although I knew about my queerness when I moved to the United States in 1999, I never talked to my colleagues and high school students about it. I was dealing with some other social issues in the community (racism and xenophobia) and I felt that it was too risky to express my sexuality in public. Pantoja Guzmán (2021) mentions how being gay and Latino in the United States includes a sense of responsibility and how we need to "double our efforts" so that our "actions speak louder than our sexual orientation" (p. 124). Also, as a Latino man, I was afraid to be rejected by my own Latinx community (Ríos Vega, 2020a). It was not until I reached my doctoral program that I had more time and space to read and to connect with individuals who were able to document and discuss how the intersection of issues of race, sexuality, immigration, language, and class shape queers of color in the United States.

CHAPTER 3

Having (Lack of) Support

Luego perdemos a nuestros padres, quienes, generalmente, menos aceptan la idea de tener un hijo marica. Algunos simplemente se sienten culpables por haber engendrado semejante réprobo de los demonios que más bien debería permanecer eternamente en las profundidades del Tártaro, o por habernos malcriado y consentido desde niños, como si eso fuera la causa de la homosexualidad.

SÁNCHEZ BAUTE, 2003, p. 71

Then we lose our parents, who are generally less accepting of the idea of having a queer child. Some simply feel guilty for having fathered such a reprobate demon that should rather remain eternally in the depths of Tartarus, or for having spoiled and spoiled us since childhood, as if that were the cause of homosexuality.

∵

In 1989, I left my mom's house to pursue higher education at age 17. Before that time, I received constant negative and sometimes toxic messages from her and my older brother. In the neighborhood, I was bullied a lot for being very effeminate or for hanging out with girls. Although I never talked to my mom about my sexuality, she caught me many times doing things associated with girls. I guessed my mother never understood that she and my older sister were my role models, so I basically emulated them. My mom always knew that I was *maricón* but did not know how to handle it. Instead, she reprimanded and punished me for doing "wrong" things. After I moved from my mom's house, finished college, and got my first teaching job, I decided to stay in Panama City until 1999 when I accepted a teaching job in North Carolina. While in the states, I started dating some guys. The second time that my mom came to visit me, Jean (pseudonym) was living in my apartment. My mom met him but never asked me about him. My relationship with Jean did not last that long. Then I started dating Chris (pseudonym). My mom met him when she flew to be part of my graduate commencement ceremony. Chris and my mom liked each other a lot. My mom met Chris's parents and sister. My mom never asked me a single question about

© JUAN A. RÍOS VEGA, 2025 | DOI:10.1163/9789004714779_003

me being gay. I always talked to her about Chris and his parents as normal. I never apologized or outed myself to her. I learned that I did not have to excuse myself for being a queer man. The fact that I left my mom's house to pursue higher education in my country and then moved to the United States allowed me to develop financial stability and respect from my mom and other relatives. It does not mean that I still have homophobic friends and relatives who do not agree with my sexuality; however, my privilege as a middle-class man, living in the United States, gives me the freedom to choose where and with whom I want to be. However, I also must acknowledge that my privilege is shared by a few LGBT individuals in Panama. Before my mother passed away in 2021, she and I talked over the phone. It was the first time that my mother talked about my LGBT writings in Panama. She shared with me that my older brother questioned her about my publications. I asked her how she responded to him and she said that no matter what I did, I was still her son. Honestly, it was the first and last time that my mother and I talked about my LGBT writings in Panama. Her comments became like a blessing for me. My mother passed away on January 1st, the same day as my birthday. Although I still and will always miss her, I feel at peace since I never hid my sexuality and my long relationship with Jean. I still talk to my older brother. Every time that I visit my mom's house, I get a chance to talk to him. He's still homophobic; however, we try to get along with each other. Losing our mom gave us a big lesson about life.

1   **Parents**

Once I knew that I liked boys and my older brother rejected me for being too *maricón,* I realized that I did not fit in in my mother's house. I always wanted to finish high school as soon as possible to leave my mother's house. Many times, after arguing with my brother, I used to cry, promising myself that one day I needed to get out of the house. Then the opportunity arrived when one of my cousins who lived in the city visited my mother's house and asked me if I wanted to move in with her parents in the city to pursue higher education. I got so excited about this opportunity. I was just 17 years old and did not have a personal identification card that made me an adult according to Panama's laws. However, I did not ask my Mom to let me go since I knew the answer would be a big no. Instead, I packed a suitcase and left for the city with my cousin. It was not an easy journey for me. Leaving my mom and siblings was not easy at all. Living with strangers was very challenging. I missed my relatives a lot, but I kept it to myself. I was afraid to let my mother know that I missed her since I knew that she would demand I go back to her house. I hid my loneliness and my queerness for a long time until I decided to move out of my cousin's parents' house during my senior year of college. I did not want my relatives to reject me for being a *maricón*.

Some of the participants in my study shared how their parents' lack of support due to their sexual orientation affected their lives. All of the participants in my study shared how they were first rejected by their parents, especially their fathers, once they knew about their sexuality. Additionally, they commented on how their mothers, although they knew about their sexuality, preferred to avoid talking about the topic. Anibal recalled when his father blamed his mother for making him a *maricón* child. His mom did not know how to handle Anibal's sexuality. Instead of supporting him, she intimidated him by creating a negative image about being gay. He shared:

> Recuerdo una cosa muy impactante para mí fue cuando mi padre una vez que yo estaba con mi mamá y mi papá, ellos estaban discutiendo, no recuerdo que estaban discutiendo. Mi papá le reclamó a mi mamá de que ella me estaba criando para ser maricón. Y eso me llamó la atención, yo era un niño y no sabía lo que estaba pasando. Pero si con el tiempo me di cuenta que yo cuando era niño era muy, muy afeminado.
>
> Mi madre también estaba bien confundida porque me decía que eso de ser gay no era bueno y que la gente no le gustaban los gays y que siempre salen en los periódicos de algún homosexual que había matado. Ella me enseñaba los periódicos y me decía, "Mira, esto es lo que les pasa a los homosexuales los matan."

> I remember a very shocking thing for me was when my father, once I was with my mom and dad, they were arguing, I don't remember they were arguing. My dad complained to my mom that she was raising me to be a "maricón." And that caught my attention, I was still a child and did not know what was going on. But over time I realized that when I was a child I was very, very effeminate.
>
> My mother was also very confused because she told me that being gay was not good and that people did not like gays and that they always appear in the newspapers of some homosexual who had killed. She would show me the newspapers and tell me, "Look, this is what happens to homosexuals, they are killed."

Cantú (2009) commented that "Homosexuals" have historically been marginalized by the dominant religious, medical, legal, and cultural discourses. Judeo-Christian religious beliefs demonized homosexuals as "sinners." Medical discourse pathologized gays and lesbians for their "sickness" (p. 34). Oscar left his parents' house once he graduated from college. He expressed how his parents, who are evangelists, used their religious beliefs to keep him away from being gay. He also shared how his father seemed to be more willing to accept his sexual orientation than his mother.

> Mis padres son protestantes evangélicos. Ellos me llevaron a encaminarme. Mi mamá en la noche cuando oraba decía, "Señor por favor libéralo de ese espíritu de homosexualidad que quiere venir a perturbar su vida." y yo escuchaba cuando ella oraba. Ella siempre tuvo la esperanza de que yo dejara de ser gay. Bueno ahora no porque yo no vivo con ella. Viví con mis padres hasta los 24 años, después me fui a trabajar. Pero esos 24 años mi mamá estuvo orando por mí. Ella sabía de mi orientación sexual. Pero cuando yo tenia como 10 años, yo no entendia eso de la homosexualidad. Fue muy complejo. Algunos pasajes de la Biblia decían que el hombre que se acuesta con hombres es abominación para Dios, entonces el Dios en el que yo creo me abomina. Eso también fue un factor que mató esa esperanza de heredar esa salvación. Lo que todo el mundo llama salvación y por esa razón yo decidí mejor apartarme de todo lo que tenga que ver con religión, porque no me está haciendo bien.

> My parents are evangelical Protestants. They led me on my way. My mom at night when she prayed, said, "Lord please free him from that spirit of homosexuality that wants to come and disturb his life." I listened when she prayed. She always hoped that I would stop being gay. Well, not now, because I don't live with her. I lived with my parents until I was 24, then I went to work. But those 24 years my mother was praying for me. She knew about my sexual orientation. But when I was about 10 years old, I didn't understand that about homosexuality. It was very complex. Some passages in the Bible said that the man who lies with men is an abomination to God, so the God in whom I believe abominates me. That was also a factor that killed the hope of inheriting that salvation. What everyone calls salvation and for that reason I decided better withdraw from everything that has to do with religion, because it is not doing me any good.

> Mi papá me decía, "Tú eres un muchacho guapo, tú eres inteligente, porque no tienes novia." Él me hacía siempre constantemente la misma pregunta y no le daba una respuesta certera, porque simplemente no tenía la independencia financiera y es un factor bastante importante, pienso que a veces uno no dice la verdad porque uno todavía está bajo

el techo de sus padres, pero cuando ya uno se siente independiente ya uno tiene voz. Le dije, "Bueno papá lo que pasa es que no me gustan las mujeres." Cuando yo le dije así, él como que reaccionó y él me dijo, "Bueno yo no lo voy a rechazar hijo porque a usted le gustan los hombres o le gustan las mujeres, usted es hijo mío y yo lo quiero tal cual como es, pero yo pienso que con su mamá sí debe reservarlo porque a su mamá sí le va a afectar bastante."

My dad used to tell me, "You are a handsome boy, you are intelligent because you don't have a girlfriend." He always asked me the same question constantly and did not give him an accurate answer, because he simply did not have financial independence and it is quite a factor. Importantly, I think that sometimes you don't tell the truth because you're still under your parents' roof, but when you feel independent you already have a voice. I told him, "Well, dad, what happens is that I don't like women." When I told him like this, he kind of reacted and told me, "Well, I'm not going to reject you son because you like men or you like women, you are my son and I love you just the way you are, but I think that with his mother if he should reserve it because his mother will be affected a lot."

Similarly, Enrique commented how his father used to reprimand him for his effeminate behavior and how his mother found love letters from another boy. He talked about how he has avoided comforting his parents about his sexuality and his relationship with Oscar. He added,

No he hablado con mis padres acerca de mi sexualidad. Incluso, bueno mi papá más que todo, es un poco homofóbico. Está cerrado a una idea como esa, porque algunas veces me ha dicho cosas bastante fuertes. Bueno, yo acostumbro a cruzar las piernas y a él no le gusta. Ha habido ocasiones en donde me ha bajado la pierna y me ha dicho, "¿por qué te sientas así? Insinuando me siento como mujer. Él sí me ha dicho de mi forma de caminar. Creo que mi apoyo principal en mi familia ha sido mi mamá. A pesar de que siempre he estado más cercano a ella nunca le he hablado de mi homosexualidad a ella. Ni ella tampoco me ha preguntado nunca nada. Pero hubo ocasiones en mi infancia en la que ella se dio cuenta de un comportamiento, así, afeminado y me llamó la atención. Uno de mis compañeros estaba tratando de llegar a mí. Él me escribía cartas de amor. Entonces ella encontró una de las cartas y me reclamó por eso. Nunca leí la carta. Ella solamente me dijo que qué era eso, qué significaba eso, que si yo había tenido algún tipo de relación sexual con él.

Pero en realidad, nunca. Tenía 11 años y estaba en 6to grado. Bueno en realidad yo me quedé callado y nunca supe que decía la carta. Sabía que el chico gustaba de mí porque ya había recibido otras cartas donde me hablaba de amor. Él también me gustaba. Nunca nos besamos, ni nada porque la relación era más que todo de compañeros de colegio. Él sigue viviendo en mi pueblo natal, pero ya incluso se casó y tiene hijos.

I have not talked to my parents about my sexuality. Even, well, my dad, more than anything, is a bit homophobic. He's narrow minded to an idea like that, because he's said pretty strong things to me sometimes. Well, I used to cross my legs and he doesn't like it. There have been times where he has lowered my leg and said, "Why do you sit like this? By hinting I sit like a woman. He did tell me about my way of walking. I think my main support in my family has been my mother. Although I have always been closer to her, I have never told her about my homosexuality. Nor has she ever asked me anything. But there was a time in my childhood when she noticed a behavior, like that, effeminate and it caught my attention. One of my classmates was trying to reach me. He wrote me love letters. So she found one of the letters and asked me about it. I never read the letter. She only told me what that was, what that meant, if I had had any kind of sexual relationship with him. But I never had anything with him. I was 11 years old and in 6th grade. Well actually I kept quiet and never knew what the letter said. I knew that the boy liked me because he had already received other letters where he told me about love. I liked him too. We never kissed, or anything because the relationship was mostly about schoolmates. He still lives in my hometown, but he's even married and has children.

Esteban and Felipe were both raised by their single mothers. However, they did not accept their sons' sexual orientation. Esteban explained how he ended up leaving his mother's house to move in with his grandmother and aunt after she realized his sexuality. He mentioned,

Mi madre casi me mata por eso. Yo con ella no tuve muy buena relación hasta el sol de hoy, ni tampoco me interesa tenerla debido a mi orient-ación sexual. A mi me crió mi abuela. Ella me dejó al cuidado de mi mamá y mi tía. Ellas me criaron y mi tía se dio cuenta de todo desde niño de todo lo que sucedió. Y ellas jamás fueron en contra mía. Siempre me defendieron ante el ataque de los demás muchachos del pueblo. Cuando me golpeaban, ellas siempre me apoyaron. Nunca fueron en mi contra.

Jamás me preguntaron por qué haces eso. Solo se preocupaban de que yo estuviera bien. Nunca hubo necesidad de hacer una confesión. Era algo que ya se sabía. Si hubo miembros de la familia que me alejaron. Después poco a poco fueron aceptando. Hay familias que hasta el sol de hoy no me hablan, pero me da igual porque ellos no pagan mis cuentas. Eso en algún momento me afectó pero luego lo superé.

My mother almost killed me for it. I did not have a very good relationship with her until today, nor am I interested in having her because of my sexual orientation. My grandmother raised me. She left me in the care of my mother and my aunt. They raised me and my aunt realized everything as a child of everything that happened. And they never went against me. They always defended me against the attack of the other boys in the town. When they beat me, they always supported me. They were never against me. They never asked me why you do that. They just cared that I was okay. There was never a need to make a confession. It was something that was already known. If there were family members who pushed me away. Then little by little they were accepting. There are families that until today do not speak to me, but I do not care because they do not pay my bills. That got to me at some point but then I got over it.

Different from Esteban, Felipe's relationship with his mother changed over time. He mentioned that after he was diagnosed with HIV+, he developed a close relationship with his mother. When I interviewed Felipe, he was studying to become a lawyer and was living with his new partner. He mentioned,

Una vez le grité a mi mamá acerca de mi orientación sexual. Enojado. Era un arranque de rabia. Le dije sabes que soy gay. Mi mamá siempre decía frases homofóbicas y eso como que me daba rabia, vergüenza más que todo. Entonces cuando se lo dije, ella entró como en un shock depresivo, pero luego de unos días cambió. Y me trató muy bien. Y hoy en día nos llevamos demasiado bien. Le dije después que tenía VIH y que necesitaba apoyo.

I once yelled at my mom about my sexual orientation. Annoyed. It was a fit of rage. I told him you know I'm gay. My mom always said homophobic phrases and that kind of made me angry, and ashamed more than anything. So when I told her, she went into depressive shock, but after a few days, it changed. And he treated me very well. And today we get along too well. I told her later that I had HIV and needed support.

During my last visit to Panama (Summer 2022), I had a chance to meet most of these men. I had a chance to ask them about their relationship with their parents (those who were still alive). Most of them said that they were getting along with their parents. Felipe was still living with his partner, and he was having a good relationship with his mother and grandmother. Oscar and Enrique were still living together in the city; however, both parents were not really accepting of their sons' sexuality. For instance, Oscar never takes Enrique to his parents' house in the countryside. Although Enrique's parents know about Oscar, he has never talked to them about his sexuality and his relationship with Oscar. There are two salient points that I want to highlight in this section—class and religion. For some families, due to their lack of education about health and sexuality issues, they tend to replicate homophobic behavior toward individuals who do not follow strict gender expectations. Sometimes it can be associated with issues of class since the public education system in Panama does not include a serious and updated curriculum that addresses issues of sexuality beyond the gender binary. In addition, religion has a controlling influence on people's interpretation of sexuality and gender performance. For instance, since the educational system is dated and Catholicism is embedded in the curriculum, LGBT individuals become victims of bullying, marginalization, and violence in schools by their classmates and teachers. Rodríguez-Doranz (2021) claims,

> While sexuality in general has been an area of human life that has been the object of social regulation, gay sexualities have been disproportionately oppressed in a way that both public and private lives have been punished. (p. 114)

Like Oscar, whose parents are middle class and highly educated, their religious beliefs force them to reject their son's sexuality. Unfortunately, students who neither have support at home from their parents and relatives nor at school end up dropping out.

2 Leaving Home

Coming out to our loved ones might be a risky step, especially when they lack serious and/or research-based literature about being gay/queer/*maricón*. Most of the time, Latinx parents prefer to avoid talking about the topic or to make negative and sometimes toxic comments about openly LGBT individuals. Those who decide to come out to their parents are sometimes disowned or kicked out of their houses. While some decide to stay with their parents and keep their sexuality a secret or conform to society's double standards, some others prefer to live their sexuality openly. In my case, I never talked to my mom about being gay. As I mentioned earlier in this text, I left her house to pursue college when I was 17 years old and never came to live in her house but to visit once or twice a year. Then, in 1999 I migrated to the United States to work as an exchange teacher. The second time that my mom came to visit, she met Jean. I never had this conversation with my mom about my sexuality and she never asked me about it. I always felt that telling my mom about my sexual orientation was like apologizing for being different. I clearly understood that my social status as a middle-class man, living in the United States, allowed me to do it. I am convinced that my situation would have been different if I were living with her without a decent job. When I asked Rodolfo about his experience with his parents about his sexual orientation, he shared,

> No fue hasta los 24 años que tuve mi primera experiencia sexual, y no fue hasta cuando se destapó la caja de pandora que mi padre me echó de casa y yo dije a la porra con la vida que he vivido.

> It wasn't until I was 24 that I had my first sexual experience, and it wasn't until Pandora's box was uncovered that my father threw me out of the house and I said to hell with the life that I have lived.

Similarly, Julio commented how he was forced to leave his foster home due to his sexual orientation. He mentioned,

> Estaba en primaria y ya no vivía en la casa porque apenas decidí decir que era homosexual, mi familia no lo tomó nada bien. Mi madre de crianza no lo tomó bien tanto que me echaron de la casa.

> I was in elementary school, and I no longer lived in the house because as soon as I decided to say that I was homosexual, my family did not take it well at all. My foster mom didn't take it well so much so that I was kicked out of the house.

Cristóbal, who comes from an upper-m family, narrated how his parents took his sexual orientation after he became a medical doctor and returned to Panama. He said,

> Cuando tenía 27 años, regresé de México después de haber estudiado medicina. Me dije a mí mismo que como estaría viviendo en Panamá por un año y que si me conseguía una pareja pues le iba a contar a mis padres.

Y pasó claro que sí. Me conseguí una pareja y le conté a mis padres. Eso fue un desastre. Bueno primero se lo dije a mamá ya que tenía más confianza con ella. Ella lloró mucho ya que no había chance de ser papá. Y entonces me fui. Yo estaba en ese entonces viviendo entre la casa de mi pareja y mi casa. Y entonces me mude a casa de mi pareja. Me deje de hablar con mi papá por un año y con mi hermana que tenía una muy estrecha relación como por tres años.

When I was 27 years old, I returned from Mexico after having studied Medicine. I told myself how I would be living in Panama for a year and that if I found a partner then I was going to tell my parents. And it was clear that yes. I got myself a partner and I told my parents. That was a disaster. Well, first I told mom since I had more confidence in her. She cried a lot since there was no chance of being a dad. And then I left. I was at that time living between my partner's house and my house. And then I moved into my partner's house. I stopped talking to my dad for a year and to my sister who had a very close relationship for like three years.

Rodolfo and Julio came from low socioeconomic backgrounds compared with Cristobal's. However, in my conversation with all of them, I realized that religion and lack of education about sexuality influenced their parents' lack of support. Both Rodolfo and Julio were kicked out of their parents' house, basically making their bodies vulnerable to a cruel society, especially when there was no parental support. Two things stand out about Rodolfo and Julio. Rodolfo was 24 years old, and still living with his parents when he was asked to leave the house. He could easily find a job to support himself; however, Julio was still in elementary school when he was literally thrown away, becoming a vulnerable child. Later, Julio shared with me how he ended up becoming a sex worker at such a young age since he did not have support from his biological parents or relatives. Cristobal's case was totally different since he came from an upper-middle-class family. Besides being a very attractive man, he was able to support himself due to his profession as a medical doctor. The last time that I met Cristobal, he shared with me why he dropped his full-time job as a doctor to become an actor, model, and entrepreneur with his sister.

3 Mental Health Issues

Being born and raised in a Latin American country comes with a lot of social expectations. Gender roles (boys and girls) are marked from day one. If you are born a boy, parents start sending messages about how many girlfriends you will have or reminding you what you are supposed to do as a boy as I mentioned before. We are not supposed to show any sign of weakness. I still recall when one of my neighbors used to call me names for being effeminate and when I told my mom about it, she said to me, "If that boy bothers you again and you do not beat him up, I will hit you when I get home." My mom's words really got me scared. The boy teased me, and I hit him on his head with a rock. I felt so proud of myself after I did it because I proved to my mom that I knew how to defend myself. My mom was not really happy about what I had done, but it was my way to please her after she reminded me about my gender expectations as a boy. I also have stories from when I started dating girls to please my mom and society. Due to my age and lack of trust in adults, I was not able to understand that I was probably dealing with a lot of mental health issues since I liked boys as far as I remember; however, I dated girls to make others believe that I was a straight boy first and then a teenager. Now, as an adult, I understand how afraid I was about my mom's and siblings' rejection to know about my sexuality although I always say that parents know who their children are, due to a homophobic society, parents tend to pretend that they don't know what is going on. No one wants to be rejected or disowned, especially by their own parents. Unfortunately, a lot of us keep our mental health issues as a personal matter and decide to hide them instead of showing any type of weakness. Although those of us who identify as gay or queer cisgender men keep perpetuating heteronormativity and machismo for not talking about mental health challenges. For instance, Oscar shared,

> Bueno me sentía rechazado, en cuanto mi autoestima, siento que fue donde mi autoestima se desmoronó totalmente yo sentía que estaba en pedazos y a veces me decía, ¿cómo yo voy a recoger los pedazos? ¿dónde estoy yo en cada uno de esos pedazos? ¿cómo sé que existo en todos los pedazos que quedan de mí? fue bastante traumático, yo llegaba a mi casa a veces y mi papá me preguntaba por qué no quería comer. Yo ya tenía 24 años. Y esto era como una secuela desde los 10 años. Todo ese proceso fue mucho a una edad tan temprana. En ese entonces pensaba que estaba solo y bueno en el salón era tan fuerte el bullying que yo sudaba, me acuerdo que mis manos sudaban frío, era tanta la vergüenza que sentía que inclusive yo no podía mirar a las personas a la cara debido al bullying. Ahora como profesor de inglés, como profesional, las cosas han cambiado. Debido a todo el bullying que pasé, decidí que si yo no tengo amigos que me apoyan, mis amigos van a ser los libros. Yo siempre fui un estudiante excelente, desde ese entonces mis notas siempre han sido A.

Well, I felt rejected, as for my self-esteem, I feel that it was where my self-esteem totally fell apart, I felt that I was in pieces and sometimes I said to myself, how am I going to pick up the pieces? Where am I in each of those pieces? How do I know that I exist in all the pieces that are left of me? It was quite traumatic; I would come home sometimes, and my dad would ask me why I didn't want to eat. I was already 24 years old. And this was like a sequel from the age of 10. That whole process was a lot at such a young age. At that time, I thought I was alone and well in the classroom. The bullying was so strong that I sweated. I remember that my hands were sweating cold, I was so ashamed that I felt that I could not look people in the face due to bullying. Now as an English teacher, and as a professional, things have changed. Due to all the bullying that I went through, I decided that if I don't have friends who support me, my friends are going to be the books. I was always an excellent student, and since then my grades have always been A.

Like Oscar, Bolívar said,

Yo vivía con mucho estado de ansiedad. Entonces, muy de niño, como a los 7 años, tuve un episodio nervioso. Recuerdo que me despertaba asustado en las noches y demás. Entonces eso afectó mi habla. Y tuve ciertos problemas de tartamudez. A los diez años mis padres me consiguieron una terapeuta de lenguaje. Años después yo me di cuenta que el problema no era físico, sino esa ansiedad grande que yo vivía. La terapeuta era mediocre. Tenía buenas intenciones y ella sí se dio cuenta. Ella sospechó de pronto de mi orientación sexual, cosa que yo no sabía. Y me acuerdo claramente de esos diez años que ella se metió en eso y me hizo sentir muy mal. Una vez ella me dijo que no fuera así. Y recuerdo muy claramente que me puse a llorar.

I lived with a lot of anxiety. So when I was a child, around 7 years old, I had a nervous episode. I remember waking up scared at night and so on. So that affected my speech. And I had some stuttering problems. When I was ten my parents found me a speech therapist. Years later I realized that the problem was not physical, but that great anxiety that I was experiencing. The therapist was mediocre. He had good intentions, and she did notice. She was suddenly suspicious of my sexual orientation, which I did not know. And I clearly remember those ten years that she got into it and it made me feel really bad. Once she told me not to. And I remember very clearly that I started to cry.

Now, as adults Oscar and Bolivar reflected on how having a lack of support at home and being bullied affected their mental health and wellbeing. Oscar's comments about being bullied as a college student was an example of how queer men's sexuality becomes questioned, especially when someone decided to become an educator in Panama. Any sign of queerness is used against you. In my case, I never talked about my sexual orientation when I was in college. I was so scared of being rejected by my peers and professors although I was infatuated with some of my male classmates. Bolivar's comments about developing speech problems is another example of how being rejected for being queer can affect not only your self-esteem but your language. Some of us are bullied and/or made fun of because of the way we talk. Boys constantly get the message that they need to speak like boys do, tough and strong. They still hear from adults and teachers things like, "Do not use your hands so much while talking," "Walk like a man," "Sit like a man," and "Dance like a man." All these toxic messages create insecurities in boys, especially if they are queer/cuir. Oscar and Bolivar are two middle-class men; however, Oscar still shows some insecurities and anxiety for being queer/cuir. He is still concerned about others' comments and reactions for being queer/cuir. On the other hand, Bolivar still has some speech problems and anxiety issues.

Unpacking Homophobia

> At the police station, they asked me if I was a homosexual and I said yes; then they asked me if I was active or passive and I took the precaution of saying that I was passive. A friend of mine who said he played the active role was not allowed to leave; he had told the truth, but the Cuban government did not look upon those who took the active male role as real homosexuals.
>
> ARENAS (1993, p. 281)

∴

One of the most interesting experiences while interviewing the participants was the fact that homophobia is usually taken for granted, especially in LGBT individuals. Most of the time it is taken as something cultural or those who claim to be oppressed are called oversensitive or made fun of. The colloquial language uses homophobic terms that associate being weak, dump, or girly. The sad thing is that this type of language is also used within LGBT communities without paying close attention to its negative connotations associated with internalized homophobia. Other instances of internalized homophobia occurred when the participants in this study excused showing affection in public to their partners as something negative or that goes against social norms. A couple of years ago, two lesbian women were arrested for kissing each other in public, becoming a public issue. LGBT groups advocated publicly for their rights to show affection and love toward their partners; however, the government did not respond to their claims. Additionally, it is important to highlight that there is a strong sense of fear of losing their jobs if they decide to talk about or express their sexuality in public spaces. As a researcher while in Panama and attending educational events during Pride month in June, I learned that transnational companies and international embassies practice laws of inclusion, especially in LGBT communities. These practices have allowed local middle-class LGBT individuals to become more visible and protected. It is very notorious when those transnational companies and embassies participate in the Pride march every June.

© JUAN A. RÍOS VEGA, 2025 | DOI:10.1163/9789004714779_004

1   Internalized

Being a transnational mariposa also allows me to analyze how I internalized homophobia since I was a child. Language has always been a powerful weapon to name individuals, and their behaviors, and associate them with being gay as something negative, offensive, and sometimes abnormal. Whenever I spoke or did something that was not socially accepted as a boy's expectation, I was reminded that I was *maricón*. I can recall how many times I was made fun of for speaking with a soft voice, crossing my legs as girls did, limp-wristing, moving my hips while walking or dancing, and even when I laughed. Now, as a researcher, I reflect on how hurtful name-calling is and how most of the time LGBT individuals internalize homophobia as the norm. There were times when I was even beat up by my brother when he did not like the way I behaved in front of him. I think that I made him feel embarrassed around his friends. Like many Latin American countries, Panama still has some State institutions where being openly gay is banned or where individuals do not feel safe to talk about their sexuality. Oscar, who is a high school English as a foreign language teacher, shared:

> Si yo agarro a mi pareja aquí en el mall podría ser hasta normal, pero uno de los mayores descontroles son las redes sociales. Ir agarrados de la mano y que alguien nos tome una foto y la publique en las redes sociales. Con el nivel de intolerancia que existe, yo no lo expondría a él ni a mi a perder nuestro trabajo, porque esa es la realidad.

> If I grab my partner here at the mall, it could be normal, but one of the biggest uncontrols is social media. Go hand in hand and have someone take a photo of us and post it on social networks. With the level of intolerance that exists, I would not expose him or me to losing our job, because that is the reality.

He added why he does not share sexual orientation with his students. He said,

> Nunca le he dicho a mis alumnos que soy gay y tengo pareja porque es bastante delicado, en especial aquí en Panamá el contexto, porque quizás no tengan la madurez, porque son estudiantes que tienen sólo 14 y 15 años, tal vez no tengan la madurez emocional, mental, de todo, para juzgar algo de esa magnitud.

> I have never told my students that I am gay and I have a partner because it is quite delicate, especially here in Panama the context, because they

may not have the maturity, because they are students who are only 14 and 15 years old, perhaps they do not have the maturity emotional, mental, everything, to judge something of that magnitude.

Finally, he criticizes effeminate guys.

El gay pride y los carnavales son dos espacios diferentes pero que se relacionan porque son la misma persona, entonces de allí los medios ponen a un hombre que no es gay a actuar y a hacer mofa de nosotros y ¿qué tenemos que hacer nosotros? Nada, porque somos partícipes de la misma pendejada. Me referí a los que son afeminados. Actuar gay es simplemente ser femenino, no sé, estar en el centro de atención donde todo el mundo te vea. No pienso que eso es ser gay, pero no sé si es una característica de la personalidad. No sé cómo definirlo, es muy complejo, al menos para mí lo es. Pienso que es por culpa de nosotros mismos, porque en todos los Gay Pride sale gente vestida como mujeres mostrando su cuerpo, besándose en público y haciendo todo tipo de actos. Creo que si tú te sientes orgulloso de lo que tú eres, tú no tienes por qué andar en un grillo en los carnavales montado enseñando, bailando y haciendo todo tipo de locuras cuando eso en realidad no es ser gay.

Gay pride and carnivals are two different spaces, but they are related because they are the same person, so from there the media put a man who is not gay to act and make fun of us and what do we have to do? Nothing, because we are participants in the same bullshit. I was referring to those who are effeminate. Acting gay is just being feminine, I don't know, being in the limelight where everyone sees you. I don't think that's being gay, but I don't know if it's a personality trait. I do not know how to define it, it is very complex, at least for me it is. I think it is our own fault because, in all Gay Prides, there are people dressed as women showing their bodies, kissing in public, and doing all kinds of acts. I think that if you feel proud of who you are, you don't have to ride on the top of a truck in the carnival showing off, dancing, and doing all kinds of crazy things when that is not really being gay.

Although Oscar actually lives with his partner, he still perpetuates homophobia toward other LGBT individuals who express their sexuality more openly. As a queer cis man, Oscar ignores his privilege while passing as heterosexual when he shares homophobic remarks about other queer people, especially during Pride and the Carnival, which is the greatest space for queer people to express themselves in Panama. Like Oscar, Juan shared how some teachers and professors who happen to be gay avoid participating in the annual Gay Pride in the city. He mentioned.

> Cuando uno es educador y gay, no puede salir del closet. Tengo amigos míos que son profesores gays y me dicen, "No voy a la marcha porque después me ven." Hasta profesores de la universidad que te dicen, "Si me ven en la marcha, van a decir que soy gay y profesor universitario."

> When you are an educator and gay, you cannot come out of the closet. I have friends of mine who are gay teachers and they tell me, "I'm not going to the march because they see me later." Even university professors who tell you, "If they see me at the march, they will say that I am gay and a university professor."

Enrique mentioned that he has never received direct discrimination for being effeminate; however, at work, he witnesses his male workers mocking being effeminate. He has also heard homophobic slurs among them but has remained quiet. Like I mentioned earlier, some LGBT individuals must choose between accepting homophobic comments as jokes or confronting the aggressors even when it means losing their jobs. Pantoja Guzmán (2021) posits how losing your job for being openly gay and asking for your rights is not "sustainable in a capitalist system" (p. 127). Unfortunately, most of them take the first option. Enrique said,

> En mi trabajo siento que todos los hombres son un poco machistas. Ellos siempre están hablando de temas homofóbicos. Bueno ellos ven muchos programas de televisión en los que salen personas gays locales, entonces ellos hablan sobre eso. Por ejemplo, ellos dicen, "Hoy en día no puedes fijarte en una mujer porque de repente puede salir que es hombre y te puedes equivocar. Puedes estar hablando de una mujer que no es." Cosas así. También se molestan entre ellos mismos con comportamientos homosexuales, pero supuestamente no lo son y lo hacen como manera de burla y con bromas homofóbicas.

> In my work, I feel that all men are a bit macho. They are always talking about homophobic topics. Well, they watch a lot of TV shows featuring local gay people, so they talk about it. For example, they say, "Nowadays you cannot look at a woman because suddenly it may come out that she is a man, and you can be wrong. You may be talking about a woman who

is not." Things like that. They also annoy each other with homosexual behaviors, but supposedly they are not, and they do it as a way of ridicule and with homophobic jokes.

It is very common to see heterosexual men teasing each other with homophobic slurs or remarks based on stereotypical TV shows or movies. Some of them shared experiences with gay people, but always kept their macho image in front of their peers. It is like they are constantly competing to show off who is more macho than the other. Also, sometimes when they know that there are some rumors that somebody that they know, maybe at work, is gay, they tend to act effeminate or tell homophobic jokes to see the gay co-workers' reaction. Since there are no laws in place to protect LGBT individuals in their workplaces, they have no choice but to accept homophobic jokes as the norm. Juan also mentioned how singing a popular song about gay men made him feel uncomfortable since he did not want people to think that he was gay. He said,

> Había una canción que me daba ansiedad en esos momentos. Era divertido pero en esos momentos me daba ansiedad. La canción decia, " marica tu, marica yo." Yo en esos momentos no quería ni cantar esa canción porque me hacía sentir incómodo delante de la gente. Me preocupaba lo que la gente iba a decir de mí si me veía cantando esa canción. Creo que ese tipo de cosas te menten en el closet más rápido.

> There was a song that made me anxious at the time. It was fun but at those times it made me anxious. The song said, "Marica you, marica me." At that time, I didn't even want to sing that song because it made me feel uncomfortable in front of people. I was worried about what people would say about me if they saw me singing that song. I think that kind of thing gets you in the closet faster.

It is important to clarify that Oscar, Enrique, and Juan identify as cis gay men, but due to homophobia and Catholicism, which are embedded in the public school curriculum and other government agencies, these men do not feel safe to express their sexual orientation openly even when their co-workers happen to know about their sexuality. It is like living in a hypocritical society, what some of them refer to as "conservative." It is like openly and stereotypically gay individuals are accepted in some spaces like beauty salons, carnivals, and to help prepare beauty pageant queens and/or to decorate Catholic images at church, but in some other spaces their queerness must be hidden; otherwise, they will be victims of discrimination for being different. It is that attitude of "keep your mariconada" to yourself. Oscar, Enrique, and Juan are socially accepted due to their middle-class status as educated individuals; however, they do not feel safe to express or share about their partners at work or with their parents. Unconsciously, all of them internalize homophobia as normal.

2   Externalized

Since Panama does not have a law that protects LGBT communities, it is almost impossible to have official records of violence against these individuals. LGBT individuals do not trust the police since some of them are their most common oppressors. Second, there is a State office called "Defensoría del Pueblo," where some cases are presented, but since the person appointed to lead that office belongs to the current political party, there is not that much that can be done since the governments have no interest in passing a hate law that specifically protects LGBT communities. Also, distance is another challenge since people who live far away from the city do not have access to report their cases. During my interviews, I learned how gay men and trans women have been victims of physical violence and ridicule in public spaces. Juan shared how he and his partner were ridiculed by an elderly woman while they were riding public transportation. He said,

> Íbamos mi pareja bajando las escaleras del metro y una señora mayor de edad iba cuatro escalones adelante. Y le digo algo a mi pareja y luego recuesto mi cabeza en su hombro. Fue un momento natural. La señora se voltea y nos grita, "Descarados, descarados." A la señora le iba a dar un infarto. "Ustedes son unos descarados." Y yo le comento a Rubén, "¿Eso es con nosotros?" Ruben estaba asustado porque a la señora le iba a dar algo. A mi no me dio por responderle nada. Así que nos quedamos callados.

> My partner and I were going down the stairs of the subway and an older woman was four steps ahead. And I say something to my partner and then I lay my head on his shoulder. It was a natural moment. The lady turns around and yells at us, "Shame on you. Shame on you." The lady was going to have a heart attack. "You guys are shameless." And I commented to Rubén, "Is that with us?" Ruben was scared because he was going to give the lady something. I did not answer anything. So we keep quiet.

Juan also shared how one of his coworkers did not get a job promotion for being effeminate. He mentioned,

Trabaje en recursos humanos en la universidad católica. Yo estaba enclosetado en ese momento cuando a un chico abiertamente gay se le cerraban todas las puertas para alcanzar un puesto más alto. La jefa de recursos humanos decía, "Él no porque él es gay y tiene que atender personas." El chico tenía todas las competencias para el cargo. La jefa era muy homofóbica y no le quería dar el puesto. Creo que eso está muy palpable en la sociedad todavía. Falta de educación. Creo que el estereotipo está ahí. El gay, el sida.

I worked in human resources at a Catholic university. I was in the closet at the time when an openly gay boy was closing all doors to achieve a higher position. The head of human resources said, "He does not because he is gay and has to serve people." The boy had all the skills for the position. The boss was very homophobic and did not want to give him the job. I think that is still very palpable in society. Lack of education. I think the stereotype is there. The gay, AIDS.

Juan's comments about his effeminate co-worker emphasize what I have been discussing previously about a hypocritical society. His co-worker was not able to be promoted due to his mannerism although he was well-qualified to do it. This practice is very common in Panama, any sign of femininity or mannerism coming from a man is questionable and scrutinized. And if the individual is a trans person, it is almost impossible to get a decent job. There is still this stigma that gay men want to be women, want to date or have sex with all men, and/or will die of aids. I will discuss these issues in the next section. This situation is even worse with trans women, who usually end up working in beauty salons or becoming sex workers. Again, there are no specific laws that protect these communities.

3   Social Media

The biggest question that I ask myself is how much social media influences homophobic and transphobic people to be violent. All the participants agreed that due to the efforts made by LGBT organizations and individuals, there is more positive visibility about them. However, some local reality shows and song lyrics still perpetuate a negative and stereotypical definition of being gay. These stereotypes are internalized by the viewers who continue defining a gay as someone who wants to become a woman, a funny person, and/or an AIDS transmitter. Anibal argues that being an effeminate gay man has always been used as a commodifier by social media, especially local TV stations. He also mentions that due to public protests and complaints by LGBT organizations and individuals, things have changed a little bit. He shared,

> Yo siento que la gente tiene la percepción de que nosotros somos tolerados en Panamá, lo cual yo siento que es cierto. Somos tolerados siempre y cuando seamos objetos de diversión. Como ciertos artistas gays que hacen reír a la gente por hacer mariconadas en televisión. Y en ese contexto la gente los tolera, porque divertimos a la gente. Pero si yo salgo en la televisión hablando de derechos hacia la población LGBT, entonces eso no es divertido. Entonces yo soy un peligro. Mire, lo que he escuchado es que el tema del gay afeminado vende. Eso divierte. Es un medio que a la gente le encanta ver ese tema de los gays afeminados. Sin embargo, lo veo tanto como lo veía antes. Yo siento que nosotros como colectivo hemos tenido mucho que ver con eso. Porque siempre tenía mucha incidencia sobre denunciar ese tipo de expresiones homofóbicas en los medios de comunicación.

> I feel that people have the perception that we are tolerated in Panama, which I feel is true. We are tolerated as long as we are objects of fun. Like certain gay artists who make people laugh by doing "mariconadas" on television. And in that context people tolerate them, because we amuse people. But if I go on television talking about rights towards the LGBT population, then that is not funny. So I am a danger. Look what I have heard is that the subject of the effeminate gay sells. That amuses them. It is a medium that people love to see the issue of effeminate gays. However, I see it as much as I saw it before. I feel that we as a group have had a lot to do with it. Because he always had a lot to do with denouncing such homophobic expressions in the media.

Similarly, Antonio added,

> Bueno yo pienso que hay muchos programas en Panamá que la moda es ser cueco payaso y todos los programas tienen un gay extrovertido, una loca que sale y con eso se burlan los supuestos heterosexuales, con lo que haga, la loca le pasa esto, a la loca le pasa al otro y esa es una forma de perpetuar la homofobia abusando bastante de eso, por lo menos programa que yo veo, La Cáscara (programa local de televisión), que ellos dicen que no son homofóbicos pero lo son, fomentan la homofobia. Infraganti (programa local de televisión) es otro programa. Es malísimo, pero está en el aire.

Well, I think that there are many programs in Panama that the fashion is to be a "cueco" and all the programs have an extroverted gay, a crazy "loca" who goes out and with that the supposed heterosexuals make fun, with what he does, the "loca" happens this, the "loca" does that, and that is a way to perpetuate homophobia by abusing it a lot, at least a program that I watch, La Cáscara (a local TV show), which they say they are not homophobic but they are, they promote homophobia. Infraganti (a local TV show) is another program. It's lousy, but it's in the ai

Cristobal referred to El Ñeque, another local show. He said,

El Ñeque nos está aplastando y criticando constantemente haciendo parodias. Y una cosa es hacer una parodia y otra cosa es hacer todo el programa de parodia hacia la comunidad LGBTQ+, lo cual no me parece.

El Ñeque is constantly crushing and criticizing us by making parodies. And one thing is to do a parody and another thing is to do the entire parody program towards the LGBTQ+ community, which I do not think.

Some of the participants in this book agreed that social media is doing a better job compared to what happened in the past. It is probably because LGBT groups have raised their voices about these types of injustices. However, I would like to discuss two things that call my attention every time I visit Panama. There are TV shows where openly gay men impersonate women. Like Anibal mentioned, these gay men sell since they perpetuate these stereotypes about being gay, a man who wants to be a woman. But to problematize these impersonators even more, they also perpetuate this idea about being a woman, a gossiper, who usually cares about fashion and makeup, who constantly talks about men, and/or the poor woman who speaks and behaves in a "funny" way. Additionally, I have seen theater performances, some of them written by gay men, where there is always an exaggerated effeminate man who makes the audience laugh with his "funny" and "stereotypical" remarks about being gay. It is like Anibal mentioned, if the gay man makes people laugh as a joker, that's totally accepted, but when the gay man speaks up or critically analyzes injustices in the LGBT communities, then that individual is not wanted anymore.

3.1   Song Lyrics

Like TV and theater performances, song lyrics contribute to stereotypes about being LBGT. In the past, popular singers, from Reggae to Panamanian folk singers have defined gay men as effeminate individuals who like to gossip, want to have sex with all heterosexual men, and/or trouble people, especially when they are at parties and get drunk. I still recall some reggae songs that literally offended gay men and how some of those lyrics were chanted loudly to oppress gay men or men who were suspicious of being gay. Rodolfo mentioned,

> Hubo una hace unos años de Samy y Sandra que se llamaba "Si tu no me has," pero era con un doble sentido porque era si tu no me has dicho que eres maricón. También hay otra de ellos mismos. La letra habla de que ella se da cuenta que el marido le era infiel y que se lo contó un amigo ñaño. Lo lamentable es que estas canciones son aceptadas culturalmente y ellos mismos como cantantes piensan que es normal. En el reggae también hay letras homofóbicas. Tenemos un cantante que es Nando Boom que ahora es pastor evangélico y tiene canciones con contenido altamente homofóbico. En sus canciones él dice que los maten, que lo apedreen, pero como son canciones populares las personas lo ven normal, lo más curioso es que los mismos gays que van a discotecas las corean y no se ponen a analizar el mensaje de la canción. Como es que un cantante de reggae pide que larguen a todos los gays de Panamá y que los maten en la canción y tú siendo gay o siendo lesbiana coreas esa canción. También están Mr. Fox y Japanese con canciones altamente homofóbicas.

> There was one a few years ago by Samy and Sandra that was called "If you have not me," but it was with a double meaning because it was if you have not told me that you are fag. There is also another of themselves. The lyrics speak of her realizing that her husband was unfaithful to her and that a friend of mine told her about it. The unfortunate thing is that these songs are culturally accepted and they themselves as singers think it is normal. In reggae there are also homophobic lyrics. We have a singer who is Nando Boom who is now an evangelical pastor and has songs with highly homophobic content. In his songs he says to kill them, to stone them, but since they are popular songs, people see it as normal, the most curious thing is that the same gays who go to discos sing them and do not analyze the message of the song. How is it that a reggae singer asks that all gays in Panama be fired and killed in the song and you being gay or being a lesbian you sing that song. There are also Mr. Fox and Japanese with highly homophobic songs.

Sammy and Sandra are famous Panamanian folk music singers and like Rodolfo mentioned they used to sing two songs where gay men were defined in very stereotypical ways. After a local LGBT organization sent them a protest letter, the singers apologized and stopped singing those types of songs. Both siblings are singers; however, Sandra has become more famous due to her particular way of dancing and the song lyrics, which usually talk about women being in love or taking revenge after being cheated by their boyfriends or husbands. I feel that it is part of the drama that most of us go through when we are in a relationship. Sammy and Sandra are very popular in Panama, especially in the LGBT community. I have seen how openly gay men like to sing Sandra's songs very loudly, and some like to attend her concerts to dance and to chat her songs, pretending to be like her. Sammy and Sandra are iconic figures in the LGBT community in Panama.

CHAPTER 5

Facing Social Challenges

In México the homosexual has many names: joto, puto, marica,
maricón, margarita, and my favorite, mariposa, butterfly, an allusion
to the feminine fluttering of eyelashes. To my mother, I was simple,
mijo. My son.

GONZÁLEZ (2006, p. 184)

∴

Although Panama has a lot of history for being a welcoming and friendly country to foreigners, those of us who are born and raised in this country and are
part of any marginalized group might have a different taste of our country.
Panama shows fewer hate crimes, especially in trans women, compared to
other Central American countries, throughout this study and personal experiences of gay men, especially, I know of gay men who were murdered due to
their sexual orientation. Some of them were my professors in college, public
figures, and professionals. As an undergraduate student, two of my professors
were killed by young guys that my professors used to date or to pay for sexual services. During the interviews, some of the participants also mentioned
how other men, usually professionals, were killed by other men; however,
those cases were never typified as hate crimes. Also, the victims' relatives usually prefer to avoid a deeper investigation of their loved ones. They might feel
embarrassed to reveal their relatives' sexual orientation as the main reason
why they were murdered. Although things have changed in the last 20 years
since I left my homeland, LGBT individuals are still vulnerable to being called
homophobic slurs, beaten up, and denied opportunities to better their lives,
especially trans women. I will talk more about the experiences of trans women
in Panama in a separate chapter.

1 Families, Friends, and Jobs

When I was living with my mother, I experienced discrimination by being
made fun of for being effeminate or for doing girls' things. Whenever I did not

© JUAN A. RÍOS VEGA, 2025 | DOI:10.1163/9789004714779_005

define what a boy was supposed to do or to be, I was called out as *maricón*. When I became an adolescent, I experienced some type of discrimination by the same boys that I had sex with. Once I moved to the city to pursue higher education, I tried to conform to social expectations as a man. Although I had sex with girls when I was in high school and college to avoid being marginalized or oppressed for being *maricón*, I still felt sexual attraction for boys and men but decided to please my mom and society.

The first time LGBT individuals receive discrimination comes from their relatives and friends. Then comes State institutions, like schools, churches, the Police Department, the Fire Department, and society at large. Oscar shared how he had experienced a lot of homophobic people in public, especially one of his cousins. He said,

> Las personas tienden a hacer gestos para indicar cuando alguien es maricón. Yo iba pasando y mi primo empezó a hacer así esos gestos y a insinuar que yo era un maricón, que yo era un marica. Me acuerdo que antes presentaban en televisión una novela que no recuerdo el nombre, pero había un homosexual que se llamaba Zaqueo. Entonces mi primo me decía, "Ahí viene el maricón de Zaqueo." Siempre que pasaba decía la misma cosa. Hace poco él puso un comentario en Facebook bastante deprimente en cuanto al Gay Pride del año pasado. Él decía que entendía como los gays pueden existir en este mundo. Yo le dije, "Mira, primero que todo tú tienes que respetar mi muro, no puedes venir a poner estupideces en mi muro, venir a ofender a personas porque tan solo tú no te sientes cómodo con las personas que están a tu alrededor. Si tú no te sientes cómodo con las personas que te rodean pues simplemente desaparece, porque obviamente van a ver muchas personas a tu alrededor que son gays, que son maricones, como tú lo llamas o qué son Zaqueos como tú me decias cuando era tan sólo un joven de 13 años." Entonces me respondió, "¿Porque tú recuerdas eso?" Y le respondí, "Porque simplemente eso que tú me hiciste se lo hiciste a un ser humano." Entonces él me preguntó, "¿Tú eres maricón? Y le dije, "Yo no soy maricón, yo soy gay y quizás soy mucho más inteligente que tú porque si tú estuvieras en mi posición, yo jamás me hubiese atrevido a poner un comentario tan despectivo. Creo que te falta bastante intelecto."

People tend to make gestures to indicate when someone is a "maricón." I was passing by and my cousin began to make those gestures like that and to insinuate that I was a "maricón," that I was a "marica." I remember that before they presented a novel on television that I don't remember the name of, but there was a homosexual named Zaqueos. Then my cousin would tell me, "Here comes Zaqueo, the "maricón." Whenever I passed he said the same thing. He recently posted a rather depressing comment on Facebook regarding last year's Gay Pride. He said he didn't understand how gays can exist in this world. I told him, "Look, first of all, you have to respect my wall, you can't come to put stupid things on my wall, come to offend people because only you don't feel comfortable with the people around you. If you do not feel comfortable with the people around you, then it simply disappears, because obviously you will see many people around you who are gay, who are 'maricónes,' as you call them or what are Zaqueos as you told me when it was just a young man of 13 years." Then he replied, "Why do you remember that?" And I replied, "Because just what you did to me you did to a human being." Then he asked me, "Are you a 'maricón?'" And I said, "I'm not a 'maricón.' I'm gay and maybe I'm much smarter than you because if you were in my position, I would never have dared to make such a derogatory comment. I think you lack quite a bit of intellect."

It is very common that when TV watchers see a gay actor on TV, they start calling somebody by the actor's name who happens to be gay or who is assumed to be gay as a joke without realizing how oppressive that might be, especially if the person is, in fact, a gay man. When I was still a child, I recall my mom's friends saying that Thursdays were "el día de los maricones" (gay men's day). When I was in my early 20s, I recall hearing relatives talk badly about gay men like if having a gay person in the family was a sin or embarrassment. One of my aunts said that she preferred her daughters to be prostitutes rather than lesbians. Although she never asked me about my sexuality, she probably knew that I was gay, so she said that aloud, so I could understand what she thought about gay people. When I shared my own experience with Oscar about my aunt's comments, he also shared how his relatives oppressed him for being *maricón* while buying lottery tickets. He said,

Otra cosa que no entiendo en el interior es que tienen la creencia en la lotería que si hablas con un maricón antes de la lotería, no vas a ganar por muchos años o no vas a ganar en ese sorteo. Nos ven hasta cierto punto como objetos de mala suerte. Lo viví con mi abuela, a pesar de que ella me quiere. Un día le iba a hablar y estaba comprando sus números y simplemente me dio la espalda y me ignoró. Yo me sentí mal y obviamente no sabía por qué era eso. Igualmente, me sucedió con otras tías. Un día se los reclamé. Les dije, "Ustedes me están ignorando porque creen que yo les voy a traer mala suerte como dicen por ahí." Desde ese momento cambiaron porque se dieron cuenta que yo sabía lo que estaba pasando.

Also another thing that I don't understand is that they have the belief in the lottery that if you talk to a gay man before the lottery you are not going to win for many years or you are not going to win in this draw. They see us to a certain extent as objects of bad luck and I lived it with my grandmother, even though she loves me. One day I was going to talk to her and she was choosing a number and she just turned her back on me and ignored me. I felt bad and obviously, I knew it was because of that, the same with other aunts and one day I told them, "You are ignoring me because you think that I am going to bring you bad luck as people say out there." And from there, they changed, because they realized that I knew what was happening.

Panama, like many other Latin American countries, has received a new wave of radical protestant churches that fight against LGBT communities, especially same-sex marriage. Due to a lack of education, a lot of individuals, especially poor individuals, perpetuate a lack of acceptance towards LGBT people. Anibal, who is the founder of the first LGBT organization in the country, shared how he was violently harassed for giving out condoms in public. He explained,

He recibido ataques homofóbicos muchas veces. Bueno recientemente tuve un problema con unos evangélicos que se encontraban conmigo en el sistema de transporte público porque no tengo automóvil. Ellos estaban predicando la palabra de Dios y me gritaban que aceptara a Cristo. En el 2008, me golpearon por repartir condones. Yo siempre me he sentido orgulloso de mi dentadura, pero se me ha ido cayendo del impacto del golpe de un puñetazo que me dieron esa vez. Casi que perdí el conocimiento del golpe que me dieron. Me empezó a sangrar la mejilla y toda la dentadura se ha movido con el tiempo. Se me han ido quebrando y cayendo los dientes. También mis vecinos me gritan a cada rato cueco, maricón, sidoso. Esto es horrible.

I have received homophobic attacks many times. Well, recently I had a problem with some evangelicals who were with me in the public transport system because I don't have a car. They were preaching the word of God and yelling at me to accept Christ. In 2008, I was beaten for handing out condoms. I have always been proud of my teeth, but they have been falling from the impact of the blow of a punch that they gave me that time. I almost lost consciousness of the blow they gave me. My cheek started to bleed and all my teeth have moved over time. My teeth have been breaking and falling out. Also my neighbors yell at me all the time, cueco, "maricón," sidoso. This is horrible.

Roberto, who is one of the youngest participants in this study, has become a public LGBT leader. During the interview, he shared how he and his partner were kicked out of Cerro Ancón, a famous historic and now tourist landmark in Panama City, by two police officers for kissing each other. Unfortunately, one of the most oppressive testimonies from LGBT individuals comes from incidents with the Police Department. Although some individuals have complained publicly about these incidents, some police officers use their religious beliefs and positions of power to discriminate and oppress LGBT communities. Roberto narrated what happened at the park. He said,

> Cuando estaba con mi novio en el Cerro Ancón, quisimos darnos unos besitos y llegó un guardia de seguridad del Estado. Nos empezó a acosar. Lo que yo hice en ese momento fue grabar. Le dije que él no tenía derecho a acosarnos y hablarnos de la biblia. Que aquí no mandaba la religión, ni la biblia y que en Panamá mandaba la constitución. Y que la constitución dice que no hay fueros, ni privilegios. Me dijo que la biblia era clara, que era hombre y mujer. Llamó a un SPI y le empezó a hacer preguntas de que él hubiera hecho si nos encontraba besándonos y el otro SPI respondió que nos hubiera esposado y nos hubiera llevado presos. Ellos nos echaron prácticamente del lugar. Nos dijeron que si no nos íbamos, nos iban a llevar presos.

> When I was with my boyfriend at Cerro Ancón, we wanted to give each other a few kisses and a state security guard arrived. He started harassing us. What I did at that time was recording. I told him that he had no right to harass us and tell us about the bible. That here religion did not rule, nor the bible and that in Panama the constitution was in command. And that the constitution says that there are no privileges or privileges. He told me that the bible was clear, that it was male and female. He called an SPI and began to ask him questions about what he would have asked if he found us kissing and the other SPI replied that he would have handcuffed us and taken us to jail. They practically kicked us out of the place. They told us that if we didn't leave, they would take us to prison.

Roberto also commented about another homophobic incident while showing the rainbow flag in public transportation. He said,

En agosto del año pasado, yo iba con una bandera en mi mochila y entonces un señor vio la bandera. El tipo me jaló por una de las cintas de la mochila. Me empujo y me empezó a golpear. Me empezo a gritar que yo era maricón y que la biblia era clara. Usaba la frase de los panameños, "Las cosas son claras en este país." Entonces en un descuido que él estaba encima mío, lo pateó entre las piernas y en ese momento cogí mi buba que es super dura y le di un golpe en su cabeza y salí corriendo como pude.

In August of last year, I was carrying a flag in my backpack and then a man saw the flag. The guy pulled me by one of the straps on the backpack. He pushed me and started hitting me. He started yelling at me that I was a fag and that the bible was clear. He used the phrase of the Panamanians, "Things are clear in this country." Then in an oversight that he was on top of me, he kicked him between the legs, and at that moment I grabbed my buba that is super hard and I hit him on the head and ran as best I could.

It is very interesting to highlight how Enrique internalized homophobia when his friends mentioned that he physically passes as a straight man, but when he talks he sounds "gay."

Mis amigas me decían, "Enrique, por fuera eres un hombre completo, tú te vistes bien como hombre, tú te ves bien, pero cuando hablas, ya, todo el mundo sabe que tú eres gay." Entonces me abstengo de hacer comentarios sobre ciertas cosas, y algunos compañeros también por respeto pienso que se abstienen de hacer comentarios cuando otros están bromeando de esa forma, y aunque no me miran a mí, en realidad, pero igual hacen comentarios homofóbicos y en son de burla.

My friends told me, "Enrique, you are a straight man on the outside, you dress well as a man, you look good, but when you speak, everyone knows that you are gay." So I refrain from making comments about certain things, and some coworkers also out of respect, I think they refrain from making comments when others are joking in that way, and although they don't look at me, actually, they still make homophobic comments and are of mockery.

Rodolfo, who is older than Enrique and has more experience as an openly gay man, critically narrated how Panama is still a homophobic country even when some mainstream individuals tend to deny it. He said,

Quien te diga que la homofobia no existe miente descaradamente. La gente dice que en Panamá no tiene homofobia, pero te lo digo por la experiencia de trabajar en una ONG del colectivo LGBT, cuando íbamos a las entrevistas y decíamos Panamá es homofóbico, los periodistas nos decían pero ustedes tienen el carnaval. Nosotros le contestamos que el carnaval es solo cuatro días y que hacemos las personas LGBT después del carnaval.

Whoever tells you that homophobia does not exist is blatantly lying. People say that in Panama they do not have homophobia, but I am telling you this from the experience of working in an NGO of the LGBT collective, when we went to interviews and we said Panama is homophobic, the journalists told us but you have the carnival. We answered him that carnival is only four days and what LGBT people do after carnival.

It is very common to hear heterosexual individuals deny homophobic incidents but to blame it on openly LGBT individuals for being made fun of or harassed. It is always the victim's fault when those incidents take place. Like in many parts of the world, the carnival represents one of the few spaces of freedom where all kinds of attendees get together to party for four or five days. In Panama, Las Tablas, a small village in the countryside, became the mecca of LGBT liberation. Unfortunately, gay men have been stigmatized by the carnival. Sometimes straight people warn their male friends, relatives, and husbands to be careful while celebrating during carnival for ending up making up or having sex with gay men. Rodolfo also gave excellent examples of externalized homophobia. He said,

Que te griten maricón o cueco a un chico en la calle o que le griten a una lesbiana tortillera, eso es homofobia, no llega al grado de violencia por dicha pero eso es homofobia.

That they yell at you "maricón" or "cueco" in the street or that they yell at a lesbian "tortillera," that is homophobia, it does not reach the degree of violence, but that is homophobia.

Since Panama lacks state laws that protect LGBT individuals from homophobic slurs and violence, most transvestite, transgender, and/or transsexuals have no choice but to drop out of school. Unfortunately, most of these individuals end up as sex workers, just a few of them get a job in beauty salons. Rodolfo mentioned,

También que a una chica trans no le quieran dar un empleo teniendo estudios eso es transfobia. Eso es negarle el derecho al trabajo. El hecho que una chica trans tenga que abandonar el colegio por el acoso de sus compañeros y de los mismos maestros, que la obliguen a dejar sus estudios y por ende tendrá que dedicarse al trabajo sexual, eso es transfobia y aunque tenga estudios, debe mentirse a sí misma y asumir una apariencia de varón para terminar sus estudios y después que los termina diga ya que terminé mis estudios voy a dejar de ser Juan para ser Mariana, pero cuando Mariana llega a buscar un trabajo puede tener todos los títulos del mundo, pero no le dan el trabajo por ser trans. Eso se llama discriminación laboral y es transfobia.

Also, they do not want to give a trans girl a job having studies that is transphobia. That is denying you the right to work. The fact that a trans girl has to leave school due to the harassment of her classmates and the teachers themselves, that they force her to leave her studies and therefore she will have to dedicate herself to sex work, that is transphobia and even if she has studies, she must lie to herself and assume a male appearance to finish her studies and after she finishes them, say since I finished my studies I'm going to stop being Juan to be Mariana, but when Mariana comes to look for a job she can have all the titles in the world, but they don't give her the job for being trans. This is called employment discrimination and it is transphobia.

Rodolfo also mentioned how while visiting a radio station during a rally to stop homophobia, he realized how the DJs had a pink button with the name "cuecometro" (gaymeter). So every time, somebody called the radio station and said or sounded homosexual, the DJ pushed that button. For the DJs, it was fun. Rodolfo said,

Estaba en una cabina de radio y tenían dos botones y uno de esos botones tenía un sonido para gays. Luego empezaron las llamadas. Había más llamadas en contra que a favor de la campaña. El botón rosado decía cuecometro. Cuando el locutor lo presionaba, se escuchaba un sonido de burla. Yo le pregunté al DJ por eso, y le dije eso se llama homofobia, pero como está culturalmente aceptado a ustedes eso le parece gracioso.

It was in a radio booth and they had two buttons and one of those buttons had a gay sound. Then the calls started. There were more calls against than in favor of the campaign. The pink button said "cuecometro." When

the announcer pressed it, a mocking sound was heard. I asked the DJ
about it, and I told him that it is called homophobia, but since it is cultur-
ally accepted to you, that seems funny.

Finally, Rodolfo manifested that most of the time, LGBT prefer not to report
homophobic incidents since they know that the police or local officials will not
protect them. On the contrary, they will become victims of homophobic ser-
mons or will be asked to repent and/ or ask for God's forgiveness. Sometimes,
politicians, religious leaders, and/or upper middle class "heterosexual" men get
involved in hate crimes while having sexual encounters with LGBT individuals;
however, due to their influences and social statuses, these incidents are not
investigated properly. Rodolfo shared a personal incident when he and his for-
mer partner had a violent incident and when visiting the local authorities, he
was reminded that he was a man and that he could defend himself and that if
he were less effeminate or gay, he would not have to deal with these types of
incidents. He shared,

> Básicamente por el tema de la homofobia y el temor a no querer ver la reali-
> dad de nuestro país, el temor de saber que ellos viven rodeados de personas
> LGBTIQ. Cuando ocurren crímenes de odio, solo por el temor y el no querer
> investigar porque puede que quien mató a la persona LGBTIQ sea una per-
> sona de alto perfil en la sociedad y tiene más sentido decir, "Él o ella se lo
> buscó por cueco o tortillera." Es más, los mismos corregidores cuando hay
> peleas de chicos o chicas y se atreven a llevar a la pareja a la ley les dicen,
> "Pero si tú eres hombre defiendete." Te lo puedo decir yo que fui víctima de
> violencia física, verbal. Si la persona que está recibiendo la violencia física
> no tiene la fuerza o la contextura para defenderse, tu crees que esa persona
> le va a devolver el golpe. Si el otro es más grande lo va a matar y él llevándolo
> al corregidor que es la primera autoridad en el municipio pensando que lo
> va a defender y viene el corregidor y le dice, "Si tu eres hombre defiendete."
> Se supone que el Estado está allí para defendernos a nosotros. El corregidor
> debe poner una multa o una boleta de alejamiento, pero te dicen que los
> dos son hombres y que no se puede hacer nada. Y te mandan para la casa.
> Por ser afeminado o maricon, te dicen que tu te lo buscaste.

> Basically because of the issue of homophobia and the fear of not want-
> ing to see the reality of our country, the fear of knowing that they live
> surrounded by LGBTIQ people. When hate crimes occur, just out of fear
> and not wanting to investigate because the person who killed the LGBTIQ
> person may be a high-profile person in society and it makes more sense

to say, "He or she asked for it because of the cueco or tortillera." It is more the same corregidores when there are fights of boys or girls and they dare to take the couple to the law they say, "But if you are a man, defend yourself." I can tell you that I was a victim of physical and verbal violence. If the person who is receiving physical violence does not have the strength or the build to defend himself, you think that person is going to strike back. If the other one is bigger, he will kill him and he will take him to the magistrate, who is the first authority in the municipality, thinking that he is going to defend him and the magistrate comes and says, "If you are a man, defend yourself." The state is supposed to be there to defend us. The magistrate must issue a fine or a withdrawal ticket, but they tell you that they are both men and that nothing can be done. And they send you home. For being effeminate or fag, they tell you that you asked for it.

Acts of homophobia are very internalized in Panama's society. It worries me tremendously when I hear homophobic language being used within the LGBT community. It is heartbreaking when I have to remind my friends that the language that they use sometimes perpetuates homophobia and transphobia. It is even more difficult for me when I have to remind my relatives that the language that they are using is offensive to me. There are many instances when my sister gets mad at me for correcting her language or when my brother tries to make fun of a man for being gay and I have to remind him that I am also gay. I still recall when one of my nephews, who happened to be drunk, referred to me as "cueco de la verga" (fucking faggot) and I counteracted his phrase by affirming my sexuality as "tell me something new about me that I don't know yet." Being marginalized and oppressed by your own kind is very hard and stressful. I can't imagine how many LGBT individuals choose to hide their sexuality from their relatives, friends, and coworkers to avoid being discriminated against, oppressed, fired, or killed.

2   Self-Discrimination

As a microcosm of Panama's society at large, LGBT individuals tend to perpetuate internalized homophobia among themselves in addition to classism, racism, and gender discrimination. Growing up in the countryside, I experienced discrimination for being very effeminate. I remember when a close relative made some comments about me as somebody who would end up dressing as a woman and getting aids. When I moved to the city to pursue higher education and to be away from my homophobic brother, I suffered discrimination for speaking Spanish with a different rhythm, which is commonly associated with low class and sometimes intelligence. As I lived with some relatives first, I tried to avoid any signs of being gay, and I am pretty sure some of my cousins figured out that I was gay.

Julio, Oscar, Enrique, and Cristobal mentioned how they have witnessed other LGBT individuals being discriminated against and how they have discriminated against other LGBT people, sometimes unconsciously. Interestingly, Julio claimed that LGBT individuals should respect each other first to ask for society's respect. He said,

> Como nosotros podemos exigir respeto, como queremos exigirle a la sociedad respétame si nosotros mismos en nuestro gremio no nos respetamos entre nosotros mismos, nos discriminamos, que no te acerques a mí porque no me gustan los gorditos, no te acerques a mí porque eres demasiado loca, no te acerques a mí porque eres transformista, no te acerques a mí porque estás muy negra.

> How we can demand respect, how we want to demand from society, respect me if we ourselves in our union do not respect each other, we discriminate against each other, that you do not approach me because I do not like chubby, do not approach me because you are too "loca," do not approach me because you are an impersonator, do not approach me because you are very black.

Oscar shared how a transgender woman was oppressed when she entered an LGBT meeting at a famous hotel. He mentioned,

> El día que estaba en la reunión en un hotel en el Casco Antiguo entró un muchacho vestido de mujer y todo el mundo se quedó mirándolo. A pesar de que todos los que estábamos allí éramos de la comunidad, todos reaccionamos extrañados. Me incluyo, y sé que estuvo mal. Nos quedamos mirando hasta que se sentó y todavía lo seguimos mirando. Se que hicimos mal, porque sabemos que debería ser aceptado.

> The day I was at the meeting in a hotel in the Casco Antiguo and a boy dressed as a woman came in and everyone stared at him. Despite the fact that all of us who were there were from the community, we all reacted strangely. I include myself, and I know it was wrong. We stared at him until he sat down and we were still staring at him. I know we did wrong, because we know he should have been accepted.

It is interesting to analyze how Enrique did not understand himself as being homophobic against effeminate gay men or trans women when he said,

> Bueno yo soy gay y no quiero parecerme a una mujer. Ciertamente hay diferencias en todas las personas, y bueno como dicen la diversidad enriquece, y a mí me ha tocado ciertamente compartir con algunas personas que se comportan más afeminados que yo, y bueno yo en mi caso no tengo problemas con eso, igual soy gay. Pero me parece que la idea de que un hombre se quiere convertir en mujer bueno no me parece del todo bien porque pienso que eres hombre, si eres gay, pero eres hombre.

> Well, I'm gay and I don't want to look like a woman. Certainly, there are differences in all people, and well, as they say, diversity enriches, and I have certainly had to share with some people who behave more effeminate than me, and well, in my case, I have no problems with that, I'm still gay. But it seems to me that the idea that a man wants to become a good woman does not seem quite right to me because I think you are a man, if you are gay, but you are a man.

During the interviews, I was able to notice how LGBT individuals can be oppressive against each other. For instance, those who do not want to be associated with openly gay men or trans women. Or those middle-class or upper-middle-class gay men who discriminate against poor, black, and/or indigenous gay men. Also, I noticed how the new wave of gay men immigrants, especially from Venezuela and Colombia have brought a more openly and diverse LGBT population in Panama. Unfortunately, some of them have shown signs of classism, homophobia, and racism, especially in Panama City where there is a large Afro-Panamanian population.

3   Double Standards

Panama's society, like many Latin American countries, pushes people to live double standards. It is very common to see people attending churches and judging others, but at the same time, they buy lottery tickets or visit casinos and some other activities that are considered sinful according to the bible. The same happens when LGBT individuals accept their sexual orientation and take the challenge to reveal it to their parents. Although parents and relatives already knew about it, they prefer avoiding talking about it. LGBT people take the risk of being disowned by their parents or to be accepted. However, those who get accepted by their parents are asked to keep their sexual orientation as a personal matter. Some of them are advised not to share it with anybody else, leaving LGBT individuals no choice but to live by double standards. Juan, Bolivar, Julio, and Raúl shared how they faced their parents when they were asked to keep their sexuality a private issue, making them feel like somebody who had broken the law. Later, I will discuss how these participants' parents' advice about their children's homosexuality is associated with religion. Juan said,

> Íbamos caminando para la casa de mi mamá y le dije quiero decirle algo. Le dije soy gay y ella no me dijo una sola palabra. Luego empecé a preocuparme pensando que le podía dar algo, un ataque cardíaco. Fue mi hermano menor quien le preguntó si estaba bien ya que yo estaba preocupado al ver que ella no decía nada. Al principio yo quería sentirme libre y mostrar mi homosexualidad, pero mi mamá me decia que no, que tenía que mantenerme quieto y no decir nada. Que nadie se tenía que enterar. Ella estaba bien asustada. Eso fue al principio, ya después lo asumió y el resto de la familia también lo entendió. Con mi papá nunca hablé directamente. Siento que se le hace muy difícil de entender. Él prefiere no saber antes de conocer un poquito. Él sabe, conoce a Rubén, mi pareja y todo, pero nunca ha tocado el tema. Para él yo soy la primera persona que vive con otro hombre.

> We were walking to my mother's house, and I told her, "I want to tell you something." I told her, "I'm gay," and she didn't say a single word to me. Then I started to worry, thinking that I could give him something, a heart attack. It was my younger brother who asked her if she was okay since I was worried when she didn't say anything. At first, I wanted to feel free and show my homosexuality, but my mother told me no, that I had to keep still and not say anything. That no one had to know. She was really scared. That was at the beginning, and later he assumed it and the rest of the family understood it as well. I never spoke directly to my dad. I feel that it is very difficult for him to understand. He prefers not to know before knowing a little. He knows, he knows Rubén, my partner and everything, but he has never touched on the subject. For him I am the first person to live with another man.

Bolivar commented how he distanced himself from his relatives when he moved to the United States when he accepted his sexuality and his family opposed it. Later, due to one of his relatives' intervention, he decided to talk to his parents when they accepted him as a gay man. He mentioned how when he came back to Panama, his family wanted to pretend that they still loved him; however, they wanted him to keep his sexual orientation private. He mentioned,

> Al principio me dijeron, "Que nosotros te amamos y no tenemos ningún problema con que tu seas gay y que tu hagas una vida gay, pero ¿por qué la gente lo tiene que saber? ¿Por qué no haces una vida sin que nadie se de cuenta de eso?" Y eso me enfureció tanto que les respondí, "Voy a mariconear todo lo que me dé la gana." Y yo creo que la gente lo escuchó y sintió tan claro que se les olvidó esa idea.

> At first, they told me "that we love you and we have no problem with you being gay and you leading a gay life, but why do people have to know? Why don't you make a life without anyone noticing that?" And that infuriated me so much that I replied, "I'm going to 'mariconear' whatever I want." And I think people listened to it and felt so clear that they forgot that idea.

It is important to mention that Bolivar is the only son in his family. He probably put his family in a tough situation since they had no choice but to accept his gay son or to lose him forever after being in the United States for 5 years. Bolivar mentioned two important social elements that make his experience a little bit different from many other LGBT individuals in Panama. His parents' strong catholic beliefs and how they had to negotiate with it. Additionally, the fact that he belonged to a middle-class family and his white skin color represented forms of privilege. He shared,

> Probablemente si no tuviera estas cosas, mis amigos del pueblo no me voltearían a mirar o se burlaran de mi en el pueblo.

> Probably if I did not have these things, my friends from my hometown would never talk to me or might make fun of me in my hometown.

Raúl mentioned about a catholic priest having sex with another man. He said,

> Si el caso de un padre en una iglesia cercana por donde yo vivo donde un compañero un amigo mío iba a tener relaciones sexuales con el padre de ahí. Si la iglesia lleva esta bandera de defender la familia tradicional. Como tú estás hablando de defender el hogar si tú atacas uno y la iglesia lo sabe. Y la mañana siguiente, el mismo padre que estaba teniendo relaciones con otro hombre levanta la copa consagrada de cristo delante de todo el mundo y se toman el vino la sangre de Cristo.

In the case of a father in a nearby church where I live, a colleague and a friend of mine was going to have sex with the father there. If the church carries this flag to defend the traditional family. As you are talking about defending the home if you attack one and the church knows it. And the next morning, the same father who was having relations with another man raises the consecrated cup of Christ in front of everyone and they drink the wine of Christ's blood.

Bolivar shared,

En Las Tablas hay una situación social bien extraña diría yo en donde se sabe que hay muchos gays y son parte activa de la comunidad. Ellos son quienes arreglan las imágenes de los santos para las procesiones, arreglan los carros alegóricos para los carnavales, pero hay un código como, "No preguntes, no digas." Es como una negación total. No se menciona la palabra gay, ni maricón, ni nada y los padres continúan hablando de sí ahí está fulano y todavía no se ha casado y todos en el pueblo saben que ese hombre no se va a casar nunca porque es maricón. Entonces hay como esta negación social de la existencia de nosotros. Esta negación está bien normalizada.

In Las Tablas there is a very strange social situation, I would say, where it is known that there are many gays and they are an active part of the community. They are the ones who fix the images of the saints for the processions, they fix the floats for the carnivals, but there is a code like, "Don't ask, don't tell." It's like total denial. There is no mention of the word gay or "maricón," or anything and the parents continue to talk about whether there is so-and-so and he has not yet married and everyone in town knows that this man is never going to marry because he is a fag. So there is this social denial of the existence of us. This negation is well standardized.

Panama as a society living with double standards is ingrained in people's idiosyncrasy. Openly gay and trans women are mostly accepted in beauty salons. Other gay men are welcome as party decorators or quinceañera party choreographers and/or dancers, float designers, and queens' dressmakers. Others decorate altars at the catholic churches to honor a saint. However, most of these individuals come from low socioeconomic backgrounds. Other gay men, like me, who belong to middle-class backgrounds have access to navigate other spaces as long as some can hide or avoid talking about their sexuality. Some of us get to internalize this form of oppression, while some others decide to risk their relatives, friends, and even jobs while living their sexuality openly. I feel that the biggest challenge that Panama's society in general has is this idea of what is being a gay person. Most of them have this idea of an effeminate man who wants to be a woman, and who wants to be penetrated by straight men.

4   Church and Politics

In the previous section, Raúl talked about catholic priests having sexual intercourse with other men as an example of double standards in Panama's society. In the past ten years, the Catholic church has been involved in scandals about priests being accused of paying male sex workers, visiting motels with other men and accused of being pedophiles. Since the Catholic church has a lot of influence and power in Panama's government, these incidents are usually ignored by Panama's society. Most of the time, those priests are removed from their churches and sent out to the countryside or overseas. In my research, I noticed that like Raúl, some of them have witnessed or had sex with catholic priests in the past. Similarly, some police officers use their position of power to benefit from LGBT individuals, especially trans women. I will discuss it more in-depth later in this book.

Julio talked about his experience in an evangelical church and how he was marginalized for being gay, especially when he challenged the pastor for being effeminate. He said,

> Cualquier persona que me hablara de Dios yo sentía que era excelente, pero apenas se daban cuenta de que era gay, la persona cambiaba su semblante. Recuerdo que cuando fui al templo evangélico. Apenas entré, yo muy afeminado para esa época, todos se me quedaron viendo como si fuera algo raro y empezaron a hablarle al pastor. Yo me quedé pensando pero qué sucede aquí. Luego llega el pastor y me dice, "Ven que te voy a sacar esos demonios de homosexualidad que tú tienes." Yo le respondí, "Yo no tengo ningún demonio, simplemente soy así." Él me dijo que no podía asistir a esa iglesia porque ahí no aceptaban a los demonios y yo me quedé que no sabía qué hacer. Cómo es que unas personas que predican a Dios, que predican amar al prójimo. Lo que en realidad están predicando es odio. Ellos me estaban juzgando simplemente por algo que soy.

> Anyone who told me about God I felt that he was excellent, but as soon as they realized that he was gay, the person changed his face. I remember

when I went to the evangelical temple. As soon as I entered, I was very effeminate for that time, everyone stared at me as if it were something strange and began to talk to the pastor. I was wondering what happened here. Then the pastor arrives and tells me, "Come, I'm going to take out those demons of homosexuality that you have." I replied, "I don't have any demons, I'm just like that." He told me that I could not attend that church because there they did not accept demons and I didn't know what to do. How is it that some people who preach God, they preach love to your neighbor? But what they are actually preaching is hate. They were simply judging me for what I am.

It seems contradictory that both institutions, the police department and the catholic church, have strict regulations that ban being LGBT; however, the same institutions cover up and/or protect individuals, especially men, who have been involved or accused of having sex with other men. In the past, when I interviewed a trans woman who was arrested and taken to a judge, she realized that the judge (a straight man) had been one of her clients in the past. The judge pretended that he did not know her and gave her a warning for being a public sex worker.

5   HIV/AIDS

En 1987, apareció el VIH/Sida y el estigma no dudó en posarse sobre nosotras. En los hospitales empezábamos a morir por falta de atención médica. Las familias nos cerraban las puertas y moríamos en silencio. Nuestros amantes empezaron a sustituir la palabra cochón por la palabra SIDA.

In 1987, HIV/AIDS appeared, and the stigma did not hesitate to settle on us. In hospitals, we were beginning to die for lack of medical care. Families closed their doors to us and we died in silence. Our lovers began to replace the word cochón with the word AIDS. (Rocha Cortez, 2022, p. 96)

As a *maricón* who survived the AIDS pandemic of the late 1980s and 1990s, I witnessed how I lost many of my friends and whether the reason why they passed was due to HIV/AIDS or not, it was always assumed that since they were gay, HIV/AIDS was the cause of their death. AIDS became a stigma, associated with being gay. Newspapers, social media, the catholic church persecuted against gay men since it was understood AIDS was contagious and it was "por culpa de los maricones" (faggots' fault). Adams (2021) shares how in the United States HIV/AIDS was initially understood as a 'gay disease.' He claims how gay teachers were not allowed to teach and instead labeled as sexual predators. Antonio, a 51 year old, a theater director and script writer, mentioned,

> Bueno primero que todo existen otros estudios muy aparte de los oficiales, que los gays es más probable que mueran atropellados por un carro. Cualquier gay muere de sida, cualquier persona puede morir de sida, a veces preguntan ¿de qué murió? dicen que murió de sida, pero no es cierto, murió de enfermedades que no tenían nada que ver con el sida, murió de tuberculosis, murió de toxoplasmosis, murió de un ataque al corazón, murió de demencia, murió de lo que sea, pero murió, porque todos aquí estamos de paso, entonces bueno eso es lo malo, pero la gente siempre dice eso, la muerte con el sida, o sea que si yo muero hoy mañana dicen se murió de sida, si se muere Pablo mañana, se murió de sida.

> Well, first of all, there are other studies, far apart from the official ones, that gays are more likely to be killed by a car. Any gay person dies of AIDS, anyone can die of AIDS, sometimes they ask, what did he die of? They say he died of AIDS, but it's not true, he died of diseases that had nothing to do with AIDS, he died of tuberculosis, he died of toxoplasmosis, he died of a heart attack, he died of dementia, he died of whatever, but he died because we are all passing through here, so well that's the bad thing, but people always say that, death with AIDS, that is, if I die today tomorrow they say he will die of AIDS, if Pablo dies tomorrow, he will die of AIDS.

It is true that many gay men, especially, tested positive for HIV, which I will talk more about in my next section; however, it was also due to a lack of responsibility from the government to support this community with the appropriate resources. Rodolfo and Felipe were diagnosed HIV positive and talked during their interviews about their experiences with homophobia and lack of education about sexuality in the country as one of the main reasons why individuals get infected by the virus. It is important to highlight that Rodolfo also worked in a non-profit that provides education and resources to individuals about HIV/AIDS and other STDs. He shared,

> Es eso que piensan que si eres gay vas a morir de sida y es algo que se creó intrínseco en lo que decían era la epidemia rosa que solo le daba a los gays, las investigaciones han descubierto que todos estamos expuestos

sin importar color, raza, clase social todos estamos expuestos a una ETS
y al VIH pero todavía a 30 años de la enfermedad todavía hay personas
en Panamá y muchos países latinoamericanos que dicen si tienes VIH es
porque eres maricón.

That is why they think that if you are gay you are going to die of AIDS and
it is something that was created intrinsically in what they said was the
pink epidemic that only gave to gays, research has discovered that we are
all exposed regardless of color, race, social class we are all exposed to an
STD and HIV but still 30 years after the disease there are still people in
Panama and many Latin American countries who say if you have HIV it is
because you are a "maricón."

Although things have changed a little bit in Panama about HIV/AIDS prevention programs, there is still a lack of knowledge and education about this
topic. Since there is not a clear sex education curriculum in Panama's public
schools, people, especially adolescents, are not aware of the consequences of
unprotected sex. Adams (2021) argues that in the United States in the 1980s
and 1990s, "Gay histories and experiences were absent from many archives,
educational curricula, and everyday conversation" (p. 62). I am hopeful that in
Panama one day, future LGBT students in the public school system will be able
to read and meet LGBT individuals whose lives can inspire them to enjoy who
they are without feeling marginalized, oppressed, and/or invisible.

Orlando Quintero (2022), activist and director of a non-profit that advocates for health programs to support sexually diverse individuals, claims that
there is a false idea that the person who lives with HIV was because it was the
individual's fault. He adds that the stigma of HIV/AIDS has decreased when it
is compared to the 1980s; however, it still hurts a lot. "People are afraid to be
isolated. There are instances when people test positive for HIV, they take their
own lives. Literally, they prefer to stop taking the antibiotics that keep them
alive" (author's translation) (La Prensa, Dec. 11, 2022). Montentegro (2022) con-
cludes that,

> HIV patients require psychological care since from the moment they
> receive their diagnosis they go through different stages of grief, not
> accepting their condition, taboo, and social and family rejection, depres-
> sion from knowing that it is a disease that has no cure." known to date,
> that their life must change, their habits must change, many times
> the sum of all these difficulties and concerns lead people to abandon
> their treatments due to the pressure they feel when being the target of

mistreatment, discrimination and violations of rights. human rights and malpractice in health care. (author's translation, p. 109)

Most parents, due to their lack of education and religious beliefs tend to avoid talking about sex and sexuality to their children since they assume that talking about it will encourage their children to be sexually active. Unfortunately, as Rodolfo mentioned, HIV/AIDS does not distinguish race, gender, and social class. He continued,

A mi se me parte el corazón que existan chicos de 15 a 25 años que sean positivos para VIH, chicos indígenas, chicos de bajos recursos, chicos con baja escolaridad. Esto me da a entender eso que al no tener la educación y tener las hormonas en el punto de ebullición se les olvida ponerse un condón y lo más triste es que si lo van a comprar y son menores de edad, no se lo quieren vender, a menos que estén a la vista y tú lo puedas agarrar, pero si es una farmacia donde los tengas que pedir al farmacéutico o farmacéutica y este sea muy conservador, te dice que eres menor de edad y no te lo quieren vender. Deberían vendérselo porque para mi el condón es acceso a la salud. Si el chico se quiere proteger, no se le puede negar su derecho.

It breaks my heart that there are boys between the ages of 15 and 25 who are positive for HIV, indigenous boys, low-income boys, boys with little education. This gives me to understand that since they do not have an education and have hormones at the boiling point, they forget to put on a condom and the saddest thing is that if they are going to buy it and they are minors, they do not want to sell it to them unless they are in sight and you can grab it, but if it is a pharmacy where you have to ask the pharmacist or pharmacist and they are very conservative, they tell you that you are a minor and they do not want to sell it to you. They should sell it to them because for me the condom is access to health. If the boy wants to protect himself, his rights cannot be denied.

Felipe, who is younger than Rodolfo, tested HIV+ in his 20s due to a lack of education. He talked about how social media sometimes perpetuates the stigma that tested positive for HIV individuals will die of AIDS. He added,

Esto es total ignorancia. Cuando voy a mis citas, veo a muchas mujeres también buscando medicamentos. Muchos hombres heterosexuales tienen el VIH, pero su machismo les impide hacerse la prueba. Luego se lo pasan a sus mujeres y a otras mujeres.

This is total ignorance. When I go to my appointments, I see a lot of women also looking for medicine. Many heterosexual men have HIV, but their machismo prevents them from getting tested. Then they pass it on to their women and other women.

Rodolfo and Felipe use their personal experiences with HIV to educate others. During my last visit to Panama, I visited Rodolfo's office and met some of his co-workers. Most of the non-profit organizations that support and educate LGBT communities receive international funds. Panama's government still lacks the appropriate resources to educate its population about sex education. Rodolfo, who travels around the country, educating regional leaders and other vulnerable communities, shared how teenagers, adults, and even children have been diagnosed with HIV due to a lack of sex education and prevention programs. The last time I saw Felipe, he was living with his partner after six years of relationship.

6   Hate Crimes

When I was pursuing my undergraduate education in Panama, I had a Spanish professor, a good looking man. Most of my female friends were infatuated with him. Mr. David (a pseudonym) was a highly educated and respected professor. There were rumors that he was gay. One of my best classmates happened to be his neighbor in a middle class apartment building. Unfortunately, during the following semester, my friend gave me the sad news that Mr. David was found dead in his apartment. Apparently, two young guys entered his apartment, killed him, and then took his car. It was said that Mr. David used to have sex with one of the guys who killed him. During my years in Panama, I learned how two others of my gay professors were killed by straight men. Some of their friends shared how the newspapers and the police department never referred to these as hate crime incidents. Since I moved to the United States, I have also known of other gay men (some of them well-known men), who have been killed by straight men. Additionally, families of the victim prefer to keep these hate crimes a secret, avoiding friends' and society's comments about their son's sexuality. Most of those investigations end up forgotten and/or filed in cabinets. As I write this section in the book, I get scared since this makes me realize how vulnerable I am every time I visit my homeland. Someone who happens to know about my sexuality or my writings can kill me, and it will never be understood as a hate crime. Instead, the state and society at large will say that it was my fault for being openly gay. Anibal mentioned,

Esto sucede porque no existe una ley como tal. El año pasado mataron a una chica trans. El cliente la apuñaló y supimos que era una mujer trans porque tengo un amigo que es fiscal y ellos estaban atendiendo el caso. El me escribió para decirme que la víctima era una chica trans. Pero no se registra como tal como porque no existe una ley contra el crimen de odio que tipifique a las personas por su orientación sexual e identidad de género, simplemente las registran por el nombre y el sexo en la cédula. Entonces no son identificadas como mujeres trans.

This happens because there is no law as such. Last year a trans girl was killed. The client stabbed her, and we learned that she was a trans woman because I have a friend who is a prosecutor, and they were attending the case. He wrote to tell me that the victim was a trans girl. But it is not registered as such because there is no law against hate crime that typifies people by their sexual orientation and gender identity, they simply register them by name and sex on the ID. So, they are not identified as trans women.

Like Anibal's comments, Oscar also shared how not having a hate crime law allows the legal system in Panama to do an in-depth investigation into individuals who are killed due to homophobia. He said,

Por ejemplo, mataron al profesor X. A él lo mataron y nunca se vinculó su asesinato con un crimen de odio, todo el mundo sabía que el profesor era homosexual, pero aquí en Panamá los medios por lo menos, nunca explicaron el caso como un crimen de odio. Pero es que aquí en Panamá no se investigan los crímenes a fondo y si no se investiga el crimen a fondo nunca se sabrá si realmente fue un crimen de odio o la persona estaba involucrada en otras cosas, pienso que el factor principal es investigar cómo se debe para llegar al punto.

For example, they killed Professor X. They killed him and his murder was never linked to a hate crime, everyone knew that the professor was homosexual, but here in Panama, at least, the media never explained the case as a hate crime. But here in Panama crimes are not investigated thoroughly and if the crime is not thoroughly investigated, it will never be known if it was really a hate crime or if the person was involved in other things, I think the main factor is to investigate how it is to get to the point.

Rodolfo added,

> Han habido tantos casos aquí en Panamá de asesinatos de personas recon-
> ocidas, que los que estamos en el tema de activismo nos dimos cuenta
> que fueron crímenes de odio, le damos los datos a los periodistas para que
> investiguen más a fondo y nos dicen que esa persona se lo buscó por andar
> buscando manachos, que se lo buscó por estar buscando tipos en una can-
> tina. Sea como sea es un crimen. Tu no le puedes decir a la víctima, "tú te lo
> buscaste" porque esa persona está muerta. Pero como vivimos en un país
> de latinoamérica, machista, conservador, donde la iglesia católica tiene
> mucho poder y donde los crímenes de odio se han normalizado.

> There have been so many cases here in Panama of murders of recognized
> people, that those of us who are on the subject of activism realized that
> they were hate crimes, we give the data to journalists so they can investi-
> gate further and they tell us that this person He was asked for it because
> he was looking for "manachos," he was asked for it for being looking for
> guys in a canteen. Either way, it's a crime. You cannot tell the victim, "You
> asked for it" because that person is dead. But since we live in a Latin
> American country, macho, conservative, where the Catholic Church has
> a lot of power and where hate crimes have been internalized as normal.

Similarly, Nandin, a Guna (indigenous tribe) trans woman, gave an example of
a Guna trans woman who was killed in 2019. She said,

> Hace un año atrás hubo un incidente en Panamá Oeste, eso es en Pacora.
> Una compañera Wigudun venía de una fiesta en la capital. Se llevó uno
> de los chicos gunas la acompañó y el chico al final estando ella en su
> casa, parece que ella vivía sola. El chico le pegó, la asaltó y la asesinó. La
> tiró al baño. Allí fue que descubrieron los vecinos por el escándalo, él
> encendió el equipo de sonido. Y entonces los vecinos sintieron eso raro.
> Fueron a verla y la encontraron muerta en el baño. Hasta la fecha el chico
> anda huyendo por todos lados. Nos enteramos que el chico se fue para
> Guna Yala a esconderse. El chico la mató a puñaladas. La envolvió en una
> alfombra y la tiró en el baño. Parece que el chico ya tenía referencias de
> violencia. Varias compañeras ya lo conocían. Como vivimos apartados
> por acá no pudimos contactar a las autoridades para darle seguimiento a
> eso. Pero todo se ha quedado allí. Sabes que aquí la burocracia es grandí-
> sima. Aún siguen investigando. En los medios salió que era un chico gay,
> y que había sido asaltado en su casa.

A year ago there was an incident in Panama Oeste, that is in Pacora. A fellow Wigudun was coming from a party in the capital. She took one of the gunas boys who accompanied her and the boy at the end, while she was at home, it seemed that she lived alone. The boy hit her, assaulted her, and murdered her. He threw it into the bathroom. It was there that the neighbors discovered because of the scandal, he turned on the sound system. And then the neighbors felt that was strange. They went to see and found her dead in the bathroom. To date the boy is on the run everywhere. We found out that the boy went to Guna Yala to hide. The boy stabbed her to death. He wrapped it in a rug and threw it in the bathroom. It seems that the boy already had references to violence. Several colleagues already knew him. As we live apart around here we could not contact the authorities to follow up on that. But everything has stayed there. You know that the bureaucracy here is huge. They are still investigating. In the media, it came out that he was a gay boy, and that he had been robbed at his home.

As you can read, the participants in this study shared how some LGBT friends and well-known people have been killed by other men, some of them lovers of the victims, and those cases were never investigated as hate crimes. Although Panama's society has become more tolerant of LGBT individuals, there is no law that protects us from being verbally or physically attacked by homophobic or transphobic individuals or groups. Our bodies are still vulnerable to anyone who is ignorance and lacks acceptance and who wants to hurt us.

CHAPTER 6

What about Trans Women?

Locas que a veces se travisten y salen a luchar la vida en las calles nocturnas de alguna ciudad necesitada de un hueco donde descargar la ira de la doble moral, un hueco que te saca la lengua de forma lasciva mientras te toca el brazo para ofertar su producto, hueco al que tal vez no le queda otra opción que mostrarse, venderse, entregarse para no sentir el vacío entre sus brazos que cada noche le quema el alma mientras camina por la acera en tacones baratos.

Locas who sometimes cross-dress and go out to fight life in the night streets of some city in need of a hole where they can vent the anger of double standards, a hole that sticks out its tongue in a lascivious way while touching your arm to offer its product, a hole that perhaps has no other option than to show itself, To sell herself, to give herself so as not to feel the emptiness in her arms that burns her soul every night as she walks down the sidewalk in cheap heels

ROCHA (2019, pp. 63–64)

∵

As a *maricón* in Panama, I never had a chance to get to know trans women before moving to the United States. I heard stories about transvestites or openly gay men. My internalized homophobia made me believe that being around effeminate men would turn me *maricón*, so I would end up cross-dressing and then die of AIDS. The irony of this was that my mother, who was an elementary school teacher, had many gay friends. Some of them used to visit her house when she organized parties or to chat with her about any school gossip. Others used to sell her clothes or shoes.

I recall my neighbors, especially men, making negative comments about other men who used to cross-dress; most of them were associated with gay men who wanted to turn into women, male prostitution, poverty, and HIV/AIDS. I learned that cross-dressed men liked to be penetrated by other men. And since they were penetrated, they performed the woman's role, the *pasivo* (passive). It made me a woman. So being around men who dress and behave as women was dangerous and contagious.

It was not until I started reading LGBT Latinx writers and doing my research studies in Panama that I learned about the trans communities. I attended meetings, events, and panels. It took me a while for the trans community to get to know me as a serious scholar. I realized that there was a totally new generation of LGBT individuals who were more vocal and brave to speak out about their experiences and to claim social justice. It was through their stories that I became inspired and empowered to continue doing my job as a transnational mariposa researcher.

Although this section is not autoethnographic, I document some of the experiences that these trans women shared through our conversations. I never felt like a girl when I was young, but many individuals thought that I wanted to become a woman due to my mannerisms and queerness. I loved to sing, dance, decorate the house, and sew. All these skills made people foresee me as a future crossdresser or transvestite. As a transnational mariposa researcher who advocates for social justice, I feel it is extremely important to include the voices of these trans women, who were labeled by their relatives and society as gay men at a certain moment in their lives. Some of them shared with me how they transitioned from assuming a gay man's identity based on social expectations and then realizing how they always felt as girls and women internally. I felt the need to echo these women's experiences in academia. Additionally, being able to attend international conferences has allowed me to gain more knowledge and to meet trans women from other Latin American countries who also inspired me to include this section in my book.

I feel very fortunate to share that these trans women allowed me to enter their lives and to document their stories full of pain, struggles, and resiliency. I must confess that there were many times when I could not even sleep after I heard their stories. I felt guilty sometimes. I hated society and questioned my own privileges as a cis-gender *maricón*. For this book, I only included self-identified trans women. Based on my observations and reflections, trans women have suffered more discrimination and violence than trans men.

1   The Girl Inside

> "I have always grown up with the mentality that I am a woman and I want to be a woman."

Lulu, Lilli Carla, Alexar, Sofia, Lulu, and Nandin were identified as boys at birth; however, as they aged, they began to self-identify and wonder about their genitals and why they did not have the same organs as the girls. Mostly and subconsciously, they began to demonstrate feminine behavior and feel attracted to boys.

Alexar tells us:

> Desde cuando tenía como 5 años, más o menos. Me atraían las cosas femeninas. Me gustaban las muñecas, los zapatos. Con mis compañeritas jugábamos con las barbies. Siempre me sentí distinta a los niños. Te digo algo, a mí me regalaban juguetes de varones y yo se los regalaba a mis hermanos porque no me gustaban. Siempre me sentí femenina. Siempre me atrajo lo de mujer.

> Since I was like five years old, more or less, I was attracted to feminine things. I liked the dolls, the shoes. With my friends, we played with the Barbies. I always felt different from other boys. I tell you something, they (parents) gave me boys' toys, and I gave them to my brothers because I didn't like them. I always felt feminine. I was always attracted to women's things.

Alexar grew up with both parents and among other boys. Seeing in her father a masculine role and receiving messages about what toys she should use and being surrounded by other boys, was not an impediment for her to continue feeling like a girl. Her parents rejected her feminine behavior from the beginning, but as she tells us, later she went through two very difficult periods: Accepting her sexuality as a gay man and then confronting and telling them of her decision to dress as a transgender woman in her adult life. Ultimately, her parents accepted her sexual orientation and gender identity. At the time of our interview, Alexar lived with her parents in the countryside.

Like Alexar's experience, Lulu explains to us,

> Yo me di cuenta de que era diferente, creo, cuando yo estaba como en kínder, en la escuela cuando en los salones de las escuelas hay cosas de niñas y de niños, que la casita y las niñas jugaban a las casitas, pero yo siempre jugaban en la casita porque me gustaba. Entonces había ropa de mujeres que a mí me gustaban y yo me ponía la ropa de mujeres porque yo quería ser la mamá de la casita y de ahí ya se me fue creando esa mentalidad de que yo quiero ser una niña, yo quiero ser una mujer.

> I realized that I was different, I think, when I was in kindergarten. I noticed that in the classrooms there were different things for girls and boys, the girls played house, but I always played house with the girls because I liked it better. So I liked women's clothes. I put on women's clothes because I

wanted to be the mother of the house. And from then, I knew I wanted to be a girl. I wanted to be a woman.

Like Alexar, Lulu, raised by both parents, always had attractive feelings toward the feminine. Perhaps at first, Lulu's parents thought that her attraction to the feminine was just a stage. However, as time passed, Lulu's inner feelings continued to grow, and she experienced her father's rejection of her. She had no other choice but to leave her house at a young age.

Nandin's childhood, her behavior towards the feminine, and the reaction of her relatives were quite different from that of Alexar and Lulu. Nandin, like Sofia, belongs to one of the native indigenous groups of Panama, Guna Yala. Most of the Guna Yala communities live on their islands on the Atlantic side and away from Panama City. But the lack of opportunities, jobs, and a better future for their children, caused the Guna population to migrate to Panama City. Although Nandin was born and raised in Panama City by both parents, they instilled Guna traditions and culture in her. She tells us about her experience of feeling like a girl since her childhood,

> Conviví con otros niños. Me atraían otros niños. Me atraían las muñecas, los juguetes de las niñas. Mi mamá se daba cuenta y me permitía todo eso. Ella me dejaba y mi papá también. Toda mi familia me dejaba, me permitían todo eso. A medida que fue pasando el tiempo en mi adolescencia, yo veía esa diferencia de trato hacia mi persona con mis compañeros que se identifican como gays, gays Latinos. Ellos me decían que no le permitían hacer esas cosas y yo decía pero porqué a mi si me permiten. Mi mamá me cuenta que desde niño me gustaban las muñecas, me gustaba compartir con las niñas. Yo me acuerdo perfectamente que cuando yo tenía 5 años, me pasaba el tiempo con mi abuela en Guna Yala y jugaba con las niñas. Yo crecí con mis primas. Normal y común. Nunca me cuestionaron. Nunca me ofendían.

> I lived with other children and was attracted to dolls and girls' toys. My mom and the rest of the family allowed me all that and my father and other relatives. As time went by in my adolescence, I saw a difference in the behavior and that it was no different from my peers who identify as gay, Latino gay. They told me that they weren't allowed to do those things, but why did they let me? Since I was a child, my mom told me that I liked dolls and wanted to share them with the girls. When I was five years old, I remember perfectly well that I spent time with my grandmother in Guna Yala and played with the girls. I grew up with my female cousins. Normal and common. They never questioned me. They never offended me.

Sofia's case, who initially identified herself as omegid, tells us how her experience was somewhat different from Nandin's. Sofia explains,

> En cuanto a mi infancia en Guna Yala fue de veras muy triste. Yo siento que así es la vida, qué puedo hacer. Fue tan triste porque mis padres, mis tíos, mis tías cuando supieron que yo era omegid, nunca me aceptaron y cada vez cuando me veían jugando con muñecas o con las niñas, siempre le decían a mis padres, mis tíos, los amigos de mi tío, le decían, "ay tu hijo es así, porque lo van dejar ser así. Yo me acuerdo de todo esto y me pegaban, se burlaban me decían, "Tú vas a ser hombre, tú no eres mujer. Tienes que cambiar tu actitud, no tienes que jugar con las niñas." Todas esas cosas me afectaron. Todo eso yo lo recuerdo. Yo siento que es muy triste para mí. Me decían, tú no eres omegid, que tú no eres mujer, que tú eres hombre. Que tú tienes pene. Que no puedes jugar con las niñas.

> As for my childhood in Guna Yala, it was really very sad. I feel that this is life, what can I do? It was so sad because my parents, my uncles, my aunts, when they knew that I was omegid, they never accepted me, and every time when they saw me playing with dolls or with girls, they always told my parents, my uncles, my friends' uncle, they told him, oh your son is like that, because they are going to let him be like that. I remember all this, and they hit me, they made fun of me, they told me: You are going to be a man, you are not a woman. You have to change your attitude; you don't have to play with girls. All those things affected me. All of that I remember. I feel that it is very sad for me. They told me, you are not omegid, you are not a woman, you are a man. You have a penis. You can't play with girls.

Unlike Nandin, Sofia received verbal and physical abuse from a very young age due to her effeminate behavior. Then we'll look at how her parents accepted her as a gay man with the condition that she did not start cross-dressing.

2   Out of the Closet

When asking the participants their opinion of the phrase "coming out of the closet," the vast majority expressed being against this expression since, as trans people, coming out of the closet was not acceptable to them. Once these bodies decide to cross-dress and accept their sexual orientation and gender expression different from the one assigned at birth, they cannot return to that closet. Lulu comments,

Me considero una chica transgénero. Bueno, desde mi infancia, desde que tengo uso de razón siempre sabía lo que quería ser y sabía lo que me gustaba, o sea, el hombre. Salir del closet para mí lo veo como una falta de respeto en el aspecto de que todavía vivimos en el tabú, en ese miedo de que si salgo qué me dirán, si salgo cómo va a aceptar la gente. Yo la verdad nunca salí del closet, yo siempre supe lo que quería ser, sin necesidad de estar en un closet, de estar ahí porque siempre demostré que yo era lo que soy hoy día.

I consider myself a transgender girl. Well, since my childhood, since I can remember, I have always known what I wanted to be, and I knew what I liked, that is, the man. In the taboo, in that fear that if I go out what will they tell me, if I go out how will people accept. I never really came out of the closet, I always knew what I wanted to be, without the need to be in a closet, because I always showed that I was what I am today.

Like Lulu, Nandin shares,

Yo le digo a las personas, "Yo nunca estuve en el closet." Expresamente siempre fui diferente a los demás. Ya consciente de que era mayor, a los 18 fue que declare públicamente mi orientación sexual. Yo nunca estuve en el closet, por eso siempre de edad, ahí fue que me declare públicamente y personalmente, especialmente con mi mamá. Ahí fue que me senté con mi mamá, "Mamá yo te quiero confesar que soy diferente. Ma' yo soy omegid." Y mi mamá dice, "Yo sé." Mi mamá tranquilamente me dijo, "Yo siempre lo he sabido Nandin. Simplemente tienes que cuidarte, te tienes que portar bien." Para nosotros, la población Guna, nunca hemos estado en un closet. Eso es lo que yo defiendo. Desde que nacemos hemos estado fuera del closet. Nuestras expresiones son tan naturales y comunes que incluso tú vas a Guna Yala y ves niños en actitudes femeninas y sencillas, naturales. Nadie los critica.

At age 18, I publicly declared my sexual orientation. I was never in the closet; that's what I always tell people. I was never in the closet. Expressly, I was always different from others. Already aware that I was of legal age, that's when I declared myself publicly and personally, especially with my mom. That's when I sat down with my mom and told her I wanted to confess that I'm different. I am omegid. And my mom says: I know. She calmly told me, "I've always known Nandin. You just have to take care of yourself; you have to behave well." For us, the Guna population, we have never been in a closet. That is what I defend. From the time we were born, we have been out of the closet. Our expressions are so natural and common that even you go to Guna Yala and see children in feminine and simple, natural attitudes. Nobody criticizes them.

It was during his trips to the Guna Yala islands that Nandin learned that the omegid are part of the Guna ancestral culture and that they represent a third gender. According to him, he tells us Guna society does not reject omegids. The omegids dress like men, but they have feminine expressions and their tasks within their homes and the Guna society are also those assigned to women. Nandin shared with us that many omegid are also dedicated to making molas, a sewing art popular among Guna women.

Like Lulu and Nandin's comments regarding the expression "coming out of the closet," Sofia pointed out that "Every human being should be free, regardless of what people will say. One has to be as one is, free." For her, coming out of the closet is like living in fear of rejection.

3   Support and Rejection

The sexual diversity in Panama crawls with prejudices and taboos ranging from the religious to the social level. Through multiple generations, it has always been the norm that to live their sexuality freely, dissident individuals had to leave their homes so as not to be a social embarrassment. Sometimes, we were disowned once our parents and relatives discovered our sexual orientation.

Since gender identity and gender performance are fluid and the access to social media, the term transgender and transsexual are relatively new in Panamanian popular imagery. Previously, mainstream society referred to a man dressed as a woman as a transvestite, a man who wanted to be a woman. For years, they also used the term *cueco*, which is derogatory and often considered an insult, to refer to effeminate or openly homosexual men and women.

As a result of this social and family rejection, many trans women have to leave their homes early and become sex workers at a very young age. Lulu tells us:

> En mi infancia la verdad hubo bajas y altas. Bajas en el aspecto de que quería vestirme de niña, pero mi papá me lo impedía. Siempre me decía, "Te hice hombre, no te hice mujer. Tú eres hombre; yo tuve un varón y no una mujer."

> In my childhood, the truth was there were ups and downs. Low in the aspect that I wanted to dress as a girl, but my dad prevented me. He always told me, "I made you a man; I didn't make you a woman. You are a man; I had a man and not a woman."

He threatened to buy her bras so she would be a woman. This caused a lot of fear in Lulu since she was very attached to her father before revealing her sexuality. Lulu only had the support and protection of her mother. At 16 and 17, Lulu began to wear blouses and women's shorts and paint her nails, hiding from her father.

> Mi papá llegó al extremo de no llevarme a barberías, él mismo me cortaba el cabello, pero tanto era la maldad que me hacía unos huecos que tenía que ponerme betún de zapatos para poderme tapar los huecos para poder ir al colegio y normal.

> My dad went so far as not to take me to barbershops, he cut my hair himself, but he was so mean that he made some holes in me that I had to put shoe polish on to cover the holes, so I could go to school as usual.

Unfortunately, Lulu's father stopped supporting her financially before she turned 18. "He doesn't talk to me anymore. He is my father, and I still love him, but he has never accepted me as I am." Although Lulu still loves and admires her father, he cannot accept her as a woman, which causes her to leave her house to become independent. In this interview, Lulu worked in a beauty salon as a stylist and attended college at night.

Similarly, Karla's story shows us how many children and young people are commonly thrown out on the street by their parents for not accepting their sexuality. It is also essential to recognize how social status and religion relate to rejection. Her parents' lack of acceptance and support pushed Karla to leave her home for the first time at age 11.

> Mis padres no aceptaban mi identidad de género y decidí irme de la casa por el maltrato físico, psicológico ... de todo. Mi papá me pegaba con la correa, con cables, con lo que encontrara. Me decía cosashorrorosas. Decía que él no quería ningún maricón y otras palabras bien ofensivas.

> My parents did not accept my gender identity, and I decided to leave the house due to the physical and psychological abuse; of everything. My dad beat me with a belt, cables, and whatever he found. He said horrible things to me. He said he didn't want any faggots and other very offensive words.

After receiving physical and verbal abuse from her father, Karla decided to leave home. Unfortunately, the night she decided to run away from her house, she was detained by the police and taken to a state institution. Her parents went to pick her up and agreed to place her in a juvenile detention center for her bad behavior. In that place, Karla finished her sixth grade of elementary school. Karla returned home once she had completed her "social integration process." Unfortunately, Karla's parents were not supportive, which pushed her to leave her home again at 14. She tells us,

> Me fui de la casa nuevamente y no sabía para dónde ir. Me tocó dormir en un parque, porque no tenía a dónde ir. Conocí a un amigo gay y él fue quien comenzó a orientarme, ayudarme. Porque yo no tenía a dónde ir, no conocía a nadie, no podía decir voy a quedarme donde mi amiga, porque de verdad no tenía a nadie. Ahí comencé a conocer todo tipo de gente.

> I left home again and didn't know where to go. I had to sleep in a park because I had nowhere to go. I met a gay friend, and he was the one who started guiding me, helping me. I didn't know anyone because I had nowhere to go; I couldn't say I would stay with my friend because I didn't have anyone. That's where I started to meet all kinds of people.

Later Karla began to dress as a woman and prostitute herself on the streets. Being on the streets from an early age has taught Karla to survive in an intolerant and cruel society. On the road, Karla learned to be independent and cunning in front of abuse from macho and abusive men. It was not until she met Don Pedro (pseudonym), founder of an organization for the rights of people of sexual diversity, that he picked her up and offered her his house as a shelter. Like Karla, Sofia had parents and relatives who rejected her for acting feminine since she was very young. Her parents tried hard to make a boy out of her by imposing masculine tasks.

> Siento que mis padres por mucho tiempo y por tantas personas que le decían: tu hijo va a hacer esto. Yo siento que como persona, como ser humano que mis padres se sentían mal porque en esa época yo era un niño, no sabía. Y como mis padres eran personas adultas, yo me imagino que mis padres pensaban, "Me da pena siempre, me dicen lo mismo. Mi hijo crecerá así cuando sea grande." Mis padres llegaron al punto de comprarme cosas de varones, pelotas, aviones, carritos. Yo no quería eso. Hasta llegó el punto de llevarme a pescar. Ir al monte. A buscar plátanos, a hacer cosas de hombre. Yo iba porque me daba miedo porque si no iba me pegaban.

My parents felt terrible because so many people told them: Your son will be this. As a human being, my parents felt bad because, at that time, I was a child; they didn't know. And since my parents were adults, I imagine that my parents thought, "I always feel sorry; they tell me the same thing. My son will grow up like this when he grows up." My parents got to the point of buying me boy things, balls, planes, cars. I did not want that. He even got to the end of taking me fishing, going to the mountain looking for bananas, and doing men's things. I went because I was scared they would beat me if I didn't go.

Sofía's father thought she would stop feeling like a girl by subjecting her to doing masculine tasks. The truth is that Sofia never stopped feeling any other way. She tells us how, from a very young age, she was already attracted to boys and how she loved to personify the female singers of the time.

Me gustaba cantar y yo no podía ver ningún árbol o una palma de coco o un río y me daba por cantar, imagino que yo cantaba las canciones de Maricela en este tiempo de los 80's. En ese tiempo ella era más famosa. Yo no podía ir al río, cantaba, me imaginaba que estaba grabando un video y cantaba. Me sentía como una mujer ya.

I liked to sing and couldn't see any tree, coconut palm, or river without singing. I imagined it was me singing Maricela's songs. It was in the '80s. At that time, she was more famous. I could not go to the river or sing; I imagined that I was recording a video and singing. I already felt like a woman.

Sofía's parents constantly scolded and hit her, and her neighbors reported when they saw her doing feminine tasks like sewing mola (colorful embroidered fabric). On more than one occasion, Sofia was kicked out of her house for not behaving according to the social expectations attributed to men.

A pesar de que me castigaban, yo nunca les hice caso. Me decían que nunca me iba a vestir de mujer, que yo era hombre. Si eres omegid está bien, pero vestido de mujer en la casa no. Te acepto omegid pero no vestido de mujer. Y yo nunca me dejaba, iba a la casa de una amiga para ir a una fiesta, un evento para poder cambiarme y cuando llegaba a la casa, me quitaba el vestido. Me quitaba el maquillaje. Poco a poco fue un proceso de mi vida, que llegue hasta donde estoy ahora mismo.

Even though they punished me, I never listened to them. They told me
that I should never dress as a woman, that I was a man. If you are omegid,
it is fine, but dress as a woman in the house is not allowed. I accept you,
omegid, but not dressed as a woman. And I never let that bother me; I
went to a friend's house to go to a party to change, and when I got home,
I took off my dress and makeup. Little by little, it was a process of my life
to get to where I am right now.

Once Sofia and her parents move to Panama City, she becomes more knowl-
edgeable about sexual identities. The contact with the Western world makes
these omegid girls adopt a trans identity.

Como Guna Yala es muy grande, hay diferentes comunidades y cada
comunidad tiene su reglamento. Yo pienso que en mi comunidad no
hay discriminación, no hay transfobia, no hay homofobia. Porque te digo
esto porque cuando me mudé a la ciudad y cuando regresé a las islas,
yo regresé vestida de mujer. Yo regresé más abierta, soy Sofía, así que
quiéranme. Y le dije a la gente, hasta al saila, a las autoridades. Y nada
pasó. A mí me han dicho compañeras que en otras comunidades ellas
no pueden vestirse de mujer. Las regañas y tienen que hacer obligatori-
amente cosas de hombre. Ir al monte y sino las multan. Yo les digo que
en mi comunidad no es así. Claro que en mi comunidad hacen cosas de
hombre. Los mandan a buscar palos o piedras pero yo voy en el grupo de
las mujeres, yo apoyo el grupo de las mujeres y a mí no me rechazan por
ir vestida en forma femenina.

Since Guna Yala is vast, there are different communities, and each community has its regulations. In my neighborhood, there is no discrimination, there is no transphobia, and there is no homophobia. I tell you this
because when I moved to the city and when I returned to the islands, I
came back dressed as a woman. I came back more open, I'm Sofia, so I
love myself. And I told the people, even the sahila and the authorities.
And nothing happened. I have been told by comrades that they cannot
dress as women in other communities. You scold them, and they have to
obligatorily do men's things. Go to the mountains, and if they don't, they
are fined. I tell them that in my community, it is not like that. Of course,
in my neighborhood, they do many things. They send them to look for
sticks or stones, but I go to the women's group; I support the women's
group, and they accept me for being dressed in a feminine way.

The interesting matter here is to understand how each island in Guna Yala has its own rules regarding sexual diversity and gender expression, in this case, accepting that women can cross-dress and be accepted on some islands. Unlike Sofia, Nandin, who is also an omegid but was born and raised in Panama City, with totally Western characteristics, tells us about his experiences as an omegid in Guna society.

> En la sociedad Guna somos prácticamente como mujeres. Y por eso coloquialmente nos llaman omegid, que literalmente se traduce "como mujer." Muchas veces se usa de una manera despectiva. En cultura Guna se nos llama coloquialmente como omegid porque precisamente nosotros somos como mujeres. Actuamos como mujeres, nos comportamos como mujeres. Tenemos un rol en la sociedad como mujer. A diferencia de las transgéneros aquí en la ciudad de Panamá y en las grandes ciudades, nosotras no nos travestismos, nosotras crecemos como varones, pero internamente somos femeninas.

> In Guna society, we are practically like women. And that's why they colloquially call us omegid, which literally translates to "as a woman." It is often used in a derogatory way. In Guna culture, we are colloquially called omegid because, precisely, we are women. We act like women; we behave like women. We have a role in society as a woman. Unlike transgender women here in Panama City and big cities, we don't cross-dress. We grow up as men, but internally we are feminine.

At the time of these interviews, Sofia looked feminine. However, Nandin looked masculine, something uncommon in patriarchal and binary countries, except for her long hair. Both identify as omegid or transgender women. More recently, trans women are educating the population about the term wigudun, the third gender in the Guna tradition.

4 Being Transvestite and Transsexual

> I think very few people understand the term trans. Some people see me as a man dressed as a woman. (Sofia)

Back in the 1960s, 1970s, and 1980s, the only name that was known to all was that a man who publicly cross-dressed as a woman was a transvestite. Everyone knew that a man who was effeminate wanted to be a woman and/or to have sex with other men. The word transvestite had a negative and even demeaning connotation. Most of the time, they were made fun of publicly, especially by heterosexual men. Sometimes they teased each other by insinuating or spreading rumors that one of them had had sex with the transvestite. Being around a transvestite was considered contagious by many. Transvestites were demonized and often persecuted, stoned, and imprisoned because "they lacked morality and positive social values." But still, many transvestites managed to resist and survive. In Panama City, an avenue known as the Fourth of July was very common, constituting a border section between the canal zone (an area protected by the US armed forces and restricted for Panamanians) and Panama City. It was common knowledge that American soldiers were the main clients of transvestites and prostitutes on the Fourth of July.

Kristi Love, Victor Miranda, and Lili Carla, who lived through total repression and persecution for going against the laws and social rules during the 1960s, 1970s, and 1980s in Panama City, tell us about the experiences of homosexuals, transvestites, and transsexuals. Kristi Love (60 years old) went from being a transvestite to transgender, Víctor Miranda (64 years old) used to cross-dress and used to be called Michelle de Panamá or Sarita Montiel, and Lilia Carla (75 years old), who represents one of the first transsexual women in Panama. In Panama, long before gay nightclubs, there were bars and cantinas where it was very common to see transvestites flirting with other men, having fun with their friends, or imitating any singer of the time.

In the 1970s, there was a bar called El Sitio, which was very famous and visited by all kinds of heterosexual people, from politicians, the military, and tourists. Although it was not a gay place, it was well known for the shows that the transvestites put on on the weekends. Kristi Love was one of the most recognized transvestites of El Sitio. She tells us what the life of a transvestite was like,

> En mis tiempos hasta para hacer un concurso de belleza, teníamos que tener mucho cuidado. Nosotros no podíamos bailar libremente como ahora. Para poder bailar en un show, en un lugar nocturno, teníamos que pasar por censura. La persona del Comité de Censura iba el día anterior y miraba cómo nos íbamos a presentar y en esa misma forma lo teníamos que presentar al día siguiente para hacer el show. Esto sucedía en los '70s. Todo era más restringido. Los concursos de belleza más lo hacíamos en las casas. Ahí nos arreglábamos y escogíamos a la reina y eso.

> When I was young, to hold a beauty contest, we had to be very careful. We couldn't dance freely like now. To be able to dance in a show, in a nightclub, we had to go through censorship. A person from the Government

Censorship Office went the day before and looked at how we were going to present ourselves. In the same way, we had to perform it the next day to do the show. In the '70s, everything was more restricted. Most beauty contests were done at home. There we got dressed and chose the queen and stuff.

Kristi comments that El Sitio was a very busy place and later changed its name to La Ruleta. "El Sitio was a pretty big bar. He had his dance floor and everything. This was not a gay place, but the gays invited straight people who liked to see the transvestite show. The word transsexual was not used, but it was a transvestite."

It is important to point out that the Panamanian State did not decriminalize homosexuality as an act of sodomy until 2008, and it was the last country in Latin America to do so. The transvestite was persecuted and arrested for not complying with the social construction of gender. In 1977, Kristy Love and another group of transvestites decided to protest at a famous radio station called El Cañonero de Don Plin to demand that the State allow them to walk freely through the streets and have their own ambient nightclubs. Kristi Love tells us:

> No fuimos vestidas de mujer totalmente porque en esos tiempos, solo si te ponías una gorra de medio lado, te amarrabas la camisa con un nudo a la cintura, un jeans, las zapatillitas o botas, que se notaba que estabas vestido diferente a un hombre te arrestaban. Como en ese tiempo era tan fuerte la batida y todo, teníamos que tener mucho cuidado. Así que nos recogimos el cabello. Cuando llegamos nos atendieron muy bien ya que eso era una emisora. Conversamos con el señor en la radio. El dio su opinión de que nosotros veníamos a buscar un espacio y que nos dejaran en nuestra discoteca y cosas así. Pero como en ese tiempo las cosas eran tan restringidas, nuestra petición no era una cosa que ellos defendían. Ellos nada más dejaron que nosotros habláramos. Cuando terminamos de hablar y abogar por nuestros derechos, salimos y a los 300 metros apareció una patrulla y nos montó a todos. Eso fue horrible. Cuando nosotros íbamos saliendo del programa, allí mismo estaban las patrullas y nos detuvieron. Nos pusieron 90 días a cada uno por escándalo en la vía pública solamente por estar vestidos de mujer en la calle. Siempre pagábamos la multa y salíamos. A los que se llevaban preso, lo metían en La Modelo (cárcel) y te cortaban el cabello.

We didn't dress totally as women. You only had to put on a half-sided cap, tie your shirt with a knot at the waist, jeans, slippers, or boots; you could tell that you were dressed differently from a man. They arrested you. Since the battering and everything were so intense, we had to be very careful. So, we put our hair up. They treated us very well when we arrived since that was a station. We talked to the man on the radio. He said that we came to look for a space and that they left us in our disco and things like that. But since items were so restricted at that time, our request was not something they advocated. They just let us talk. When we finished speaking and advocating for our rights, we went out, and after 300 meters, a patrol appeared and mounted us all. That was horrible. When we left the program, the patrols were right there, and they arrested us. They gave us 90 days each for the scandal on public roads, just for being dressed as a woman on the street. We always paid the fine and left. Those who were arrested were taken to La Modelo prison and cut their hair.

We could rescue this as one of Panama's first public struggles for sexual diversity. "We fought back a lot so that the new generations have it easier," said Kristy Love. Unfortunately, the existence of a law that penalized homosexuality as a form of public scandal and a lack of morality and positive social values made these feminized bodies much more vulnerable to harassment and social rejection. Another element against him was religion, mainly Catholicism, which condemns homosexuality as an act of sodomy. Likewise, relatives of homosexuals were criticized by society. This made many, especially men, leave their homes to not be a disgrace to the family. On many occasions, middle and upper-class families sent their homosexual children abroad so that the whole family would not be victims of "what will they say."

Despite the social rejection, Kristi Love and another group of transvestites decided to hold a beauty contest to choose a queen to represent them during the carnival in 1978.

Cuando yo gané el concurso de la reina del carnaval. El tema era La Jaula de las Locas y Karla (otra travesti) había sido la ganadora y yo quedé de primera finalista. Y al ver que Karla no podía salir porque tuvo muchos problemas con la familia, yo si pude agarrar la corona. Y quedé como la reina del carnaval. Se comentaba que iba a haber carro alegórico y todo el mundo estaba esperando un carro alegórico de la Jaula de las Locas, pero ese carro nunca iba a salir. Solamente era un comentario para alegrar los carnavales. En esos tiempos si el carro alegórico hubiera salido, eso hubiera causado muchos problemas, porque la gente no estaba tan acostumbrada como ahora. Lo único que hicimos fue ir a la Avenida Central y allí me senté con la corona y todo. Ahí estaban las damas y todo.

Entonces cuando ya se estaba poniendo como muy escandaloso, que la gente estaba como muy desatada, los policías nos aconsejaron que era mejor que nos fuéramos para nuestras casas. En mis tiempos a los homosexuales les tiraban piedra desde los balcones. Pero siempre había gente que te apoyaba.

When I won the carnival queen contest, the carnival troupe theme was La Jaula de las Locas (The Birdcage), and Karla (another transvestite) was the winner, and I was the first runner-up. And seeing that Karla couldn't go out because she had many problems with the family, I was able to grab the crown. And I was like the queen of the carnival. It was announced that there would be a float, and everyone was waiting for the float Jaula de las Locas, but that car was never going to come out. It was just a comment to cheer up the carnivals. In those days, if the float had come out, that would have caused many problems because people were not as used to it as they are now. The only thing we did was go to Central Avenue, and there I sat with the crown and the women around. So when it was getting really scandalous, when people were really unleashed, the policemen advised us to go home. Those days, they used to throw stones at homosexuals from balconies. But there were always people who supported us also.

More than social acceptance of sexual diversity, there has been social morbidity in Panama. Transvestites were often victims of ridicule and fun, proving they were not socially accepted. In a misogynistic and heteronormative society, being a woman shows weakness. And the fact that a man was not only effeminate but also dressed as a woman, he suffered much more discrimination and rejection by society, especially in public places. Being openly homosexual in those days was extremely risky. Kristi Love recalls:

Recuerdo también que un día estábamos haciendo una compra y unas patrullas les dio por llevarnos. Éramos como 6 y a los 6 nos agarraron y nos condenaron pero nos dieron chance (oportunidad) de que uno fuera a pagar la multa de todos. Solamente por estar en la calle y parecer homosexual te llevaban. La razón que ellos decían por los arrestos era escándalo en la avenida pública.

I also remember that one day we were shopping, and some patrols decided to take us away. We were like 6, and the six of us were caught and sentenced, but they gave us a chance (opportunity), and one of us went out to pay the fine. They took you away just for being on the street and looking like a homosexual. The excuse for detaining us was that we were a scandal to the public.

Víctor Miranda was a well-known and somewhat controversial figure in the 70s. He was the first to open a gay nightclub called La Maxim in Panama City when homosexuality was still considered a crime. For going against the law, the police arrested and accused Victor that his nightclub was the main reason many homosexuals stayed out in the city's principal streets, especially on weekends. Victor tells us:

> Los gays de antes eran diferentes en el sentido de que eso estaba prohibido. Y yo me aventé a abrir la primera discoteca gay y me llevaron preso a la corregiduría de Bella Vista porque decían que había proliferación de homosexuales por la Vía España. Tú no sabes todo lo que yo pase. Acuérdate que lo prohibido siempre es lo que la gente busca. Como no había otro lugar a donde ir, la gente iba y eso se llenaba a morir.

> Gays from before were different in the sense that it was forbidden. And I threw myself into opening the first gay nightclub, and they took me to the Bella Vista police quarter because they said there was a proliferation of homosexuals along the Vía España. You don't know everything I go through. Remember that the forbidden is always what people are looking for. Since there was no other place to go, people went, and it was always packed to the top.

Apart from being the owner and manager of La Maxim, Víctor also cross-dressed, becoming Michelle from Panama, Sarita Montiel. He performed as Sarita Montiel, a famous Spanish singer, without effort, in his own real voice.

> Yo era quien abría los eventos. Yo era el presentador. Yo mismo hacía todo. Era muy famosa. Todavía estoy esbelta y todavía me puedo arreglar de nuevo. La loca más famosa que tuvo este país fui yo y todavía estoy viva.

> I was the one who opened the events, and I was the host. I did everything myself, and I was very famous. I'm still slim, and I can still fix myself again. This country's most famous crazy woman was me, and I'm still alive.

Those who saw Sarita Montiel said that her beauty and voice were extraordinary, and listening to her sing was like seeing a real woman. Similar to Kristi Love's comments, Víctor tells us that it was forbidden to be cross-dressed in public places and that just being mannered or cross-dressing as a woman was an excuse to be taken to jail. But inside the disco, same-sex couples danced.

> Yo sí me vestía de mujer porque yo era la dueña del local y la presentadora, pero dentro del local. Cuando salía de allí me quitaba todo y salía normal. El que era gay tenía que serlo de manera oculta. Antes era horrible. Sólo se vestían de mujer cuando iban a actuar en el show. Te vestías en el camerino y hacías tu show. Cuando salías del camerino, te vestías de hombre. Si te veían en la calle actuando afeminado la patrulla te llevaba y eso era todo.

> I dressed as a woman because I was the place's owner and the host but inside the business. When I left there, I took everything off and came out normal. The one who was gay had to be so in a hidden way. Before, it was horrible. They only dressed as women when they would perform in the show. You dressed in the dressing room and did your presentation. When you left the dressing room, you dressed as a man. If they saw you in the street acting effeminate, the patrol would take you, and that was it.

For several reasons, Lili Carla's story is quite different from those of Kristi Love and Victor. Lili Carla decided to undergo a sex reassignment operation in the early 1980s, becoming one of the first transsexuals in Panama. Even though she tried to have her surgery done in Panama, the local doctors refused. As a result, Lili Carla traveled to Colombia to make her dream come true. She tells us:

> Pasé un año de terapia psicológica. Eso no fue tan rápido. Y no depende de lo que tú pareces, sino de lo que tú tienes dentro. En la terapia me preguntaban, "Este,¿te podemos decir el femenino de tu nombre?" y yo pregunté ¿por qué?" y me dijeron, "No es solo una prueba." Y yo acepté. En vista de que ellos me pusieron el femenino, entonces empezaron a decirme Carla en la terapia más que Lili. Entonces me puse Lili Carla.

> I spent a year of psychological therapy. That was not so fast. And it doesn't depend on what you look like, but on what you have inside. In treatment, the therapists asked me, "Um, can we call you by your feminine name?" and I wondered why? and they told me, "It's not just a test." And I accepted. They began to call me Carla in therapy more than Lili. Then I started to use Lili Carla.

Lili Carla's masculine name was Carlos, so she included Lili before Carla to avoid remembering her masculine name.

Eso fue en 1985. Me da risa porque cuando llegué a Colombia, yo tenía mi pasaporte de hombre, pero eso ya estaba viejo y yo de tanto tomar hormonas ya había cambiado. Cuando llegó al counter de Bogotá, la colombiana tuvo que enseñarle los papeles de mi cambio y la cosa, hasta que finalmente entendieron. Tanto fue la espera dando explicaciones que perdí el avión de regreso para Panamá. Me tuvieron que conseguir vuelo en otra aerolínea para poder regresar. Cuando llegue a Panamá, tuve que explicar al hombre de migración lo de mi cambio de sexo.

That was in 1985. It makes me laugh because I had my man's passport when I arrived in Colombia, but it had already expired. Also, I looked different after taking so many hormones. When I arrived at the counter in Bogotá, the Colombian woman who helped me had to show her my papers about my surgery and all the stuff until they (the counter staff) finally understood. The matter took so long that I missed the plane back to Panama. They had to get me a flight on another airline to be able to return. When I arrived in Panama, I had to explain to the immigration man about my sex change.

Once in Panama, Lili Carla has the help of a gay friend who works at the hospital, and he is the one who helps her heal after her surgery. While in the apartment of her "gay mother," Lili Carla decided to go to the Electoral Court to change the name on her identity card.

Aproveché y fui a cedulación, porque hay una ley en Panamá, donde aceptaban, porque nosotros estábamos primero que muchos otros países. En aquel entonces habían mujeres de Argentina, Chile y de por allá operadas que andaban con documentos de hombres porque no les habían cambiado la ley.

I took the opportunity and went to the identification registrar's office because there is a law in Panama where we were accepted because our country was ahead of many others. At that time, there were women from Argentina and Chile who had been operated on and still had their men's documents because the law had not changed.

The law to change the name on the identity card needed to be verified by many documents from doctors and psychologists as proof that the person had undergone sex reassignment. But this did not reduce people's morbidity. Lili Carla commented how once she was able to change the name on her identification card, she was the victim of comments and sneering in the streets when she was recognized by people.

Cuando baje allí donde se retira la cédula, yo veo el cuchicheo y la cosa. Y yo me paro así, muy hermosa como tú me viste ahí (en la foto). Yo vi el tiqui, tiqui, y pregunté, "Oiga hay algún problema?" y respondieron, "No, no, no." Les dije, "Bueno, cualquier cosa que quieran saber, díganme. Si quieren que les enseñe otra cosa, se las enseño." "No, no disculpe." Me respondieron. Como evitando confrontación.

When I came down from where the identity card was withdrawn, I noticed the whispering. And I stood, very beautiful as you saw me there (in the photo). I saw people gossiping about me, and I asked, "Hey, is there a problem?" They answered, "No, no, no." I told them, "Well, tell me anything you want to know. If you want me to show you something else, I'll show it to you." "No, don't excuse me." They answered me to avoid confrontation.

Before her operation, Lili Carla had already taken hormones and was cross-dressing. It was very common to have parties and meetings at other friends' houses since, at that time, as Víctor commented, there were no gay nightclubs in Panama City. So transvestites and homosexuals created their own recreation spaces. It was very common for gays and transvestites to visit bars and bars for heterosexual audiences. Lili Carla said:

La primera cantina donde llegué a Calidonia estaba detrás del Teatro Encanto. Allí había un barcito donde se metían todos los gays. Eso era pecado. Hacían batidas y todos nos teníamos que esconder. Se llamaba Rincón Romántico. Después de allí, al frente del Teatro Encanto, en toda una esquina estaba La Chalet, donde íbamos todos los gays. Llegaba la policía y con una servilleta te limpiaba y si tenías maquillaje, pa' dentro, pa'l Alacrán, que en ese tiempo le decían al carro de la patrulla El Alacrán. Eso era horrible.

The first bar where I arrived in Calidonia was behind the Teatro Encanto. There was a little bar there where all the gays hung out. That was a sin. They would raid, and we all had to hide. It was called The Romantic Corner. Across from Teatro Encanto, on a whole corner, was La Chalet, where all of us gays used to go. The policemen would come and clean you with a napkin. If you had any makeup on, go into the patrol car called El Alacrán. That was horrible.

Like Kristi Love and Victor, Lili Carla points out that police repressed and penalized homosexuality, causing them to hide from the police. If the police

arrived at any place and found men with some makeup on their faces, it was
enough to incarcerate them in a cell commonly known as *La 50*.

> Nadie podía estar maquillado. Había una que se maquillaba y la cosa
> pero simplemente si se te notaba que eras maricón, ibas pa' lla', hasta
> que alguien te sacara y pagaras la multa. Ser maricón era el pecado más
> grande.

> No one could wear makeup. One put on makeup and stuff, but if it was
> noticed that you were a maricón, you went there until someone took you
> out, and you paid the fine. Being a maricón was the greatest sin.

The police commonly oppressed and punished homosexuals and transvestites. On many occasions, when they were in bars and canteens, and the police
entered, they had to hide in the back of the establishment or in the warehouses
used to store merchandise. Lili Carla commented:

> Cuando venía la policía nos encerraban en el depósito donde guardaban
> las cajas para que no nos llevaran. Nos protegían los que trabajaban en el
> bar. Porque nosotros íbamos a gastar. Esto pasó en 1965, y yo tenía 21 años.

> When the police came, they locked us in the warehouse where they kept
> the boxes so they wouldn't arrest us. We were protected by those who
> worked in the bar since we used to spend our money there. This hap-
> pened in 1965 when I was 21 years old.

Law and the police kept control and punished homosexuality. Besides that,
many individuals in society also verbally and physically abused any individual
who appeared to be homosexual, either because they were cross-dressing or
because they looked effeminate. Lili Carla continues:

> Una vez cuando pasaba por El Marañón (barrio popular) ví como a una
> loca partida la correteaban y le tiraban palos y piedras. Yo no lo leí, lo
> viví. Simplemente porque parecías maricón te correteaban como un
> maleante.

> Once when I was passing through El Marañón (a famous neighborhood),
> I saw how a loca partida (openly effeminate gay man) was being chased
> around, and they threw sticks and stones at him. I didn't read it; I lived it.
> Simply because you looked like a maricón, they chased you like a thug.

Presumably, Lili Carla looked like a transvestite in Panamanian society, which was enough of an excuse to be harassed. She tells us that she was once persecuted by a group of individuals simply for wanting to demand her rights as a person of sexual diversity.

> Salí en el periódico. Para ese día, estaban anunciando que iba a ver una concentración de los gays, que no los dejaban vivir y no sé qué cosa. Hace como 50–52 años. Me voy pa' allá, pa' la cuestión y cuando voy a ver, y no llegaron las locas a hacer ninguna manifestación y yo estaba allí. Yo llegué vestidita de hombre pero se me notaba, yo ya tenía (se toca los pechos) y viene un periodista y se me acercó y comenzó la vaina. La gente estaba protestando y me venían a pegar. Me trate de esconder en la tienda delChino y este me dice, "Aquí no, tú eres problema." Y cuando salgo así, Dios siempre me pone en el camino personas que me dan la mano. Cuando en eso veo un taxi viejo. Un tipo que manejaba el carro, un moreno, me dice, "Vente, vente, que te voy ayudar. Súbete." Me subí al taxi y la gente detrás gritando cosas. Me iban a acabarrr. Me monté al taxi. Me siguieron hasta la Avenida B como para matarme. De dónde salió ese taxi, dónde me dejó, si pagué o no pagué, no me acuerdo. Aquel hombre me salvó del problema. Eso fue un milagro.

> I was in the newspaper. For that day, they were announcing that I would see a concentration of gays, that they wouldn't let them live, and I don't know what. About 50–52 years ago. I'm going there, for that matter, and when I go to see, the maricón didn't come to make any demonstration, and I was there. I arrived dressed as a man, but he could tell I already had (he touched his breasts). A journalist came and approached me, and the sheath began. People were protesting, and they came to hit me. I tried to hide myself in an Asian man's grocery store, but the owner told me, "Not here; you're a problem." And when I go out like this, God always puts people in my way who give me a hand. I saw an old taxi. A guy who was driving the car, a dark-haired man, tells me, "Come on, come on, I'm going to help you. Get on." I got into the taxi, and the people behind me were yelling things. They were going to finish me. I got into the cab. They followed me to Avenue B as if to kill me. Where did that taxi come from, where did it leave me, if I paid or not, I don't remember. That man saved me from trouble. That was a miracle.

Documenting and analyzing when homosexuality was still legally penalized in Panama is essential. There was already a law from 1974 allowing the General

Directorate of Identification of the Electoral Court to change sex and gender for transgender people who could check for sex reassignment. This Law 100 of 1974 was restructured by Law 31 of 2006 and is still in force. Panama was the third country to accept name changes on identity cards for transgender people.

Our investigations do not clarify how Panama allowed transsexual people to change their names on their identity cards after proven sex reassignment. Still, at the same time, there was a law from the 1940s that criminalized homosexuality. During our interviews with Lili Carla, she also told us about an upper-middle-class homosexual who was very famous among homosexuals and transvestites of the time, whom we will call Raúl Victoria (pseudonym) to protect her identity.

> Yo conocí a Raúl Victoria. Era alto flaco, perfilado. Su familia vivía en El Cangrejo, eran de negocios y la cosa. Raúl era gay, partidísimo (muy afeminado), campeón de natación en El Club de Yates y Pesca, donde iban los rabiblancos (familias adineradas de Panamá). Pero a él le gustaba ir al mercado público donde había otra cantina llamada La Salsa. Recuerdo que nos cerraban una cantina y nos metíamos en otra. Y yo era del grupo de ballet y después de los ensayos, en grupito, siempre íbamos todos juntos, y Raúl llegó allí. A él le gustaba ir donde estaban los carretilleros. A él le gustaba tener sexo con los carretilleros. No le importaba ser rabiblanco de El Cangrejo (barrio de clase media y alta). Él se ponía caderas falsas, en un pantaloncito corto se metía trapos para hacerse caderas porque era demasiado delgado. Pero cantaba opera como tú no tienes idea. En ese tiempo la cédula era en blanco y negro y se cumplía la mayoría de edad a los 21 años. Y viene la loca y cayó presa antes de los 21 y tuvo que ir la tía, porque el papá no quiso ir. Yo era de Catedral (barrio popular en aquel tiempo) pero a él le gustaba estar con nosotros. Nosotros íbamos a esas áreas porque era allí donde los maricones podíamos respirar un poco. A Raúl le decían Elizabeth Taylor, porque era hermosa y se ponía a cantar ópera en la cantina. Eso era algo ma-ra-vi-llo-so. Después que cayó preso y salió en los periódicos, agarró un cuarto por Catedral y se casó con una puta, no sé si fue pa' recibir la herencia. Yo lo visitaba en su apartamento. La loca pintaba con la ópera y la cosa. Tenía talento. Él era un artista nacional. Luego sus padres hicieron el parapeto y lo mandaron para España. Eso era ser maricón en ese tiempo, ya sea de abolengo o de allá abajo.

> I met Raúl Victoria. He had a tall, skinny, delicate profile. His family lived in El Cangrejo; they were in business and stuff. Raúl was gay, very effeminate, swimming champion at the Club de Yates y Pesca, where the

rabiblancos (wealthy families from Panama) went. But he liked to go to the public market where there was another bar called La Salsa. I remember that they closed a canteen for us and we went into another. And I was part [of] the ballet group, and after rehearsals, in a small group, we always went together, and Raúl arrived there. He liked to go to [where] the fruit cart vendors were. He wanted to have sex with them. He didn't mind being a rabiblanco from El Cangrejo (middle and upper-class neighborhood). He put on fake buts; he put on rags to make buts because he was too skinny in shorts. But he sang opera like you have no idea. At that time, the identity card was in black and white, and he reached the age of majority at 21 years. And he was caught by the police before he was 21, and his aunt had to go because his father didn't want to go. I was from the Cathedral (a popular neighborhood at the time), but he liked being with us. We went to those areas because that was where we faggots could breathe a little. Raúl was called Elizabeth Taylor because she was beautiful and he used to sing opera in the bar. That was something wonderful. After he was imprisoned and appeared in the newspapers, he took a room in the Cathedral and married a whore; I don't know if he went to receive the inheritance. I visited him in his apartment. The crazy lived for opera and that stuff. He had talent and was a national artist. Then his parents made the parapet and sent him to Spain. That was being a maricón at that time, whether you belonged to the middle class or were poor.

Panama City has always had iconic places where significant historical events took place, which were later considered safe spaces for communities of sexual diversity. Places like Vía España, The Fourth of July, Calidonia, Santa Ana and El Casco Antiguo. And *maricones*, transvestites, transsexuals, and prostitutes frequented these three areas, where there were many canteens and bars. It was widespread to see politicians, lawyers, professors, and some hidden homosexuals mixing with homosexuals and transvestites and often having a good time in those spaces or perhaps ending up in a motel or at the home of one of the two. Even today, The Old Town and several of its bars are places frequented by people of sexual diversity. Several have changed their names over the years, but their clientele remains the same. I remember visiting many of those places, like La Madrid, La Chinito, and La Calientita, when I was still studying.

Kristi Love, Víctor, and Lili Carla have agreed on recognizing that the new generations have had a less oppressive path than the one they had to live. All indicate that it is much easier for today's society to accept a person of sexual diversity than in their youth. However, even though no law penalizes homosexuality and effeminate men, some are arrested and forced to pay fines, and institutionalized discrimination occurs against people of sexual diversity (Ríos Vega, 2018, 2020b).

5   We Are Trans Women

Panamanian society has had difficulty understanding new terms of sexual and gender identities, products of capitalism, social networks, and the migration of people. Panamanians who have freely lived and experienced their sexuality abroad return with challenging thoughts and knowledge against the "norm" or a new generation of sexually-diverse individuals who copy identities from other countries such as the United States, Spain, and other European countries. For example, Lulu, Nandin, Carla, and Sofía develop new sexual identities due to their geographic mobilization within Panama or the influence of social networks. Lulu tells us,

> Cuando tenía más o menos 15 años, decidí aceptar mi identidad de género. Al principio no conocía las palabras transexual y transgénero. Yo me sentía que era mujer, una niña, porque todavía no conocía esa terminología y yo siempre decía; yo soy una mujer, soy una niña, pero los términos los vine conociendo ya a los 19 años cuando empiezo a entrar en las redes sociales, ya existían creo, que uno podía entrar y ver bien, y de ahí me fui empapando.

> When I was about 15 years old, I accepted my gender identity. At first, I did not know the words transsexual and transgender. I felt that I was a woman, a girl, because I still did not know that terminology, and I always said: I am a woman, I am a girl, but I came to know the terms when I was 19 years old when I began to enter social networks, they had already existed, I think, that one could enter and see well, and from there I knew better.

Like Lulu, many other trans women have learned to adopt a transgender identity through the Internet. However, in this case, Lulu makes a difference between what it is to be a transvestite and what it is to be transgender based on the opposite identification of the gender assigned at birth and her female gender expression.

> Al principio hubo varios términos y yo dizque no me siento así, incluso un tiempo llegué a sentirme travesti, porque no me vestía todos los días de mujer. Solo era por ocasiones, pero siempre andaba muy afeminada,

pero yo me decía, no esto no es lo mío, lo mío es 24/7 y ya me fui metiendo en la cabeza que yo era una transgénero y no una travesti.

At first, there were several terms, and I didn't feel that way; I even felt like a transvestite for a while because I didn't dress as a woman every day. It was only for occasions, but I was always very effeminate. Still, I told myself, no, this is not my thing; mine is 24/7, and I was already getting into my head that I was transgender and not a transvestite.

Nandin, for his part, also tells us about his transition from identifying as a gay man first, then omegid. Then, after contacting an association for the rights of people of sexual diversity, he assumed an identity as a transgender woman.

A los 18 años empecé el activismo LGBT gracias a la Asociación Hombres y Mujeres Nuevos de Panamá con Ricardo Beteta (activista local) quien me invitó. Por él fue que empecé a aprender todos estos conceptos y yo me identificaba como gay, yo decía yo soy un gay indígena. Pero después que empecé yo a descubrir mi identidad, yo me dije, "Nandin tu no eres gay, tú eres una persona transgénero. Allí fue que empecé a decirle a mi gente en Guna Yala, no, nosotros no somos gays, nosotros somos transgéneros. Para el mundo occidental, nosotros somos transgéneros, somos personas trans. Si bien es cierto somos varones, por naturaleza somos varones, pero socialmente venimos creciendo como mujeres.

At the age of 18, I started LGBT activism thanks to the Asociación Hombres y Mujeres Nuevos de Panamá with Ricardo Beteta (local activist), who invited me. Because of him, I began to learn all these concepts, and I identified myself as gay; I said I am an indigenous gay. But after I started to discover my identity, I said to myself, "Nandin, you are not gay; you are a transgender person. It was there that I began to tell my people in Guna Yala, no, we are not gay; we are transgender. In the Western world, we are transgender. We are trans people. Although we are indeed men, by nature, we are men, socially, we have been growing as women.

It is imperative to analyze the case of the trans women of Guna Yala. Nandin tells us two important points. First, the figure of a third gender exists in the Guna culture known as omegid, which represents a man with feminine characteristics and functions within the Guna society and is accepted. Second, omegid people do not cross-dress as women on the islands; they recognize themselves as omegid by their mannerisms and feminine tasks within the home. However, Nandin points out that once omegid migrate to Panama City, they begin to cross-dress.

> En la ciudad se ha aumentado la cantidad de omegids vestidas de mujer. Ha habido un aumento de travestismo en la comunidad omegid pero a principios del siglo XXI, ya eso no se veía. Nosotros nos vestíamos como varones porque así crecimos, femeninas pero vestidas como varones. Pero cuando migramos a la ciudad, la gran cantidad de omegids que migraron a la ciudad comenzaron a adquirir los comportamientos y las prácticas del mundo occidental entonces empezaron a travestirse y es por eso que la mayoría de las omegids aquí en la ciudad de Panamá son travesti, la mayoría, pero si te vas para Guna Yala, allá te vas a encontrar con omegids que ni siquiera se travisten. Están vestidos de hombre.

> In the city, the amount of omegids dressed as women has increased. There has been an increase in cross-dressing in the omegid community. Still, that was no longer visible at the beginning of the 21st century. We dressed like men because that's how we grew up, feminine but dressed like men. We migrated to the city, and many began to acquire the behaviors and practices of the Western world. They began to cross-dress, and that is why most of the women here in Panama City are transvestite, most of them. Still, if you go to Guna Yala, you will find some omegids who don't even know the term transvestite. They are dressed as men.

As a manifesto of Nandin's testimonies regarding how people adopt a trans identity when they arrive in Panama City, Sofía tells how she began to cross-dress once she met other omegid people who already did, thus assuming the term transgender and not transvestite, as Nandin mentioned above.

> Pero tanto que estuvo en mí la decisión de ser trans, lo que yo sentía, lo que yo quería ser. Comencé a conocer a personas mayores que yo que eran ya eran personas trans. Comencé a convivir con otras chicas trans omegids porque yo veía que ellas tenían un cuarto de alquiler. En este tiempo había tres personas trans omegid. Vivían en un cuarto de alquiler. Casi cerca de mi casa mis padres consiguieron un cuarto de alquiler. Cada vez que me mandaban para la escuela no iba a la escuela; me quedaba donde ellas. Ya la influencia que yo veía me gustaba más y dejé la escuela.

> I decided to be trans because that was in me; that was, I felt I wanted to be. I started meeting people older than me who were already trans people. I started living with other trans omegid girls because I saw that

they had a room for rent. At that time, I met three trans omegid people. They lived in a rented room. Very close to my parents' house, I got a room to rent. Every time they sent me to school, I didn't go; I stayed with my omegid friends. I liked being around my omegid friends, so I dropped out of school.

Meeting other people from the Guna community in Panama and feeling identified as omegid helped Sofia accept that she was not just omegid but that her sexual identity is a transgender woman in the Western world. We should note her parents consider an omegid as long as she continues to dress as a man. As stated before, this is so in most of the Guna Yala islands. But Sofía, identifying herself as a transgender woman, decides to start cross-dressing, hiding from her parents.

Lo que yo iba al tiempo de hacer mi vida. Me sentía más identificada. Me sentía libre. Y no me importó que mis padres me regañaran, me pegaran, me llamaran la atención, no me importó. A los 12, 13 años quería ser yo, no quería estar vestida de hombre. Quería tener el cabello largo, quería maquillarme. Quería verme femenina. Entonces comencé a ver a mis amigos, a personas de mi misma edad, yo pensé, yo no sabía la terminología trans. Yo no sabía trans, yo solo sabía que era omegid, que era muy diferente. Después yo decidí sola. Yo soy omegid y me gusta ser así, maquillada, y sentirme femenina y decidí vestirme de mujer a escondidas de mis padres. Iba a la casa de una amiga y me vestía allá. Me sentía en libertad. Aunque no tenía cédula, iba a fiestas, a bares de omegid vestida de mujer desde los 13 años.

I felt free. And I didn't care if my parents scolded me, hit me, or called my attention, I didn't care. At 12, 13, I wanted to be myself. I didn't like to be dressed as a man. I wanted to wear long hair, to make up and look feminine. Then I started to see my friends, other people of my same age. I didn't know the trans terminology. I didn't know what trans was; I knew I was omegid, that I was very different. Then I decided by myself: I am omegid and I like to be like that, made up, be feminine and I decided to dress behind my parents' back. I went to a friend's house and dressed there. I felt freedom. I went to parties, omegid bars dressed as a woman when I was only thirteen, and I didn't have an identity card.

Although Karla has always been attracted to children since her childhood, it was not until she was 17 years old that she realized that she was not gay but a trans woman and began to dress as a woman all day.

No soy gay, soy una chica trans. Bueno yo era gay porque me vestía de hombre, pero sentía cosas como una mujer, me sentía mujer. Yo veía otra trans y yo decía; yo quiero estar así. Me gustaba y me llamaba la atención eso, y yo sé que eso me gustaba. Al principio tuve una confusión, tuve como una ... que no sabía, después tuve que ir a una psicóloga y ella me explicó, y allí fue donde me di cuenta más porque ella me abrió más la mente. Entonces he decidido, porque en realidad soy así, soy trans. Desde niño me sentí niña.

I am not gay; I am a trans girl. Well, I was gay because I dressed as a man, but I feel myself as a woman. I observed other trans girls and I wanted to be just like that. I liked it and it caught my attention and I knew it was what I liked. In the beginning, I was confused. I had like a ... I didn't know. I visited a psychologist and she explained and opened my mind. Then I could make my mind up because, to tell the truth, I'm that, I am trans. Since childhood, I have felt like a girl.

We can point out that Sofía, Nandin, Lulu, and Karla first went through a stage of acceptance when they realized they had felt like girls since childhood. After internalizing that they were gay men since they liked men. However, it was having contact with other transgender women when they realized that they are not gay, nor do they feel like transvestites, but trans women. In the case of Sofía and Nandin, migration is part of this situation. Nandin learns that within the Guna culture, there is a figure of a third gender commonly called omegid, and later, she knows the term wigudun. For her part, Sofia understood that she was a woman before she moved to Panama City, but her contact with other women who cross-dressed and identified as trans women allowed her to adopt a new gender identity. After this acceptance, Sofía changed her gender identity and expression as a transgender woman, but she also identifies as a wigudun within the Guna culture. This sexual identity and gender expression as transgender women add other types of oppression towards Sofia and Nandin, who, like other ethnic groups, are victims of racism and discrimination.

The narratives of trans women have impacted my life tremendously as somebody who belongs to the LGBT community, but also as someone who enjoys some types of privileges such as cis-gender identity and class. Toward the end of last year (2023) news spread around the country when a trans woman called Estrellita was beaten up to death by her customer, a construction worker. This incident, as many others that relate to *maricones*, brings visibility to this marginalized community, but also a lot of homophobic comments and ignorant opinions. LGBT organizations organized vigils to bring attention to the entire country about the vulnerability of trans women in Panama. I was in Panama right after the incident happened. Unfortunately, although people protested this type of hate crime, laws have not changed at all. Trans women continued being harassed and marginalized in Panama's society. Estrellita survived the atrocities of her client; however, she will live the rest of her life as a paralyzed individual in bed and taken care of by her mother and sister in a poor neighborhood in Panama's countryside.

CHAPTER 7

A Hopeful Transnational Mariposa

Él me vio mirándolo y se dio cuenta que yo había descubierto su casual erección. Se puso como un tomate, trató de dar vuelta, intentó taparse con la parka, pero el tumulto se lo impedía. Estaba tan incómodo con esa punta de unicornio delatando que, para tranquilizarlo, le brindé una sonrisa cómplice.

He saw me looking at him and realized that I had discovered his casual erection. He turned like a tomato, tried to turn around, tried to cover himself with his parka, but the tumult prevented him from doing so. He was so uncomfortable with that unicorn tip giving away that, to reassure him, I gave him a knowing smile.

LEMEBEL (2020, p. 158)

∴

Panama's geographical position has welcomed individuals from all walks of life. Those who visit from nearby countries in Central America see Panama as a modern and safer place, especially for LGBT communities. On my last trip to Panama, I met foreigners from Venezuela, El Salvador, and Colombia who shared that they could live their sexuality in Panama more openly than in their homelands. As somebody who has lived in the United States for over 20 years, I can see how open and vocal new generations are about their sexuality. Twenty-five years ago, I used to attend the first LGBT meetings in a hotel. I remember how my friends and I had to enter the hotel like criminals since we were afraid of being arrested for having a gay men's meeting. Some of my friends were afraid that their parents knew about their sexual orientation.

Although things seem to be much better now, I still miss how my generation navigated gay spaces, such as La Calientita, La Madrid, Pasos, Boys' Bar, Meto's Bar, and Los Caracoles, in a homophobic society. I stayed for over a month in the summer of 2022. Since it was Pride Month, I also took the opportunity to visit some gay places, to reconnect with and meet new friends. In addition, I lectured about my new book in Spanish about *Testimonios LGBTIQ+ in Panama*. Honestly, I visited most of the gay dance clubs in the city with some friends. I went to Envy, a middle-class gay dance club in Via España, downtown Panama. The place

© JUAN A. RÍOS VEGA, 2025 | DOI:10.1163/9789004714779_007

reminded me of those fancy gay clubs in South Beach, Miami, and Key West. I realized that the entrance fee was very high for most locals, so the place became very classist. Two things caught my attention in this place. First, people did not dance in couples like my friends and I used to. Second, the drag shows started at 2 or 3 in the morning. Although the place looked nice and I had a wonderful time with my friends, I learned that it was a very cliquish space for gays. I had promised Raúl to stop by the gay dance club where he performs on weekends. I was told that the place called Lips was very seedy since it was on the outskirts of the city. I convinced a friend of mine to take me there since I wanted to give Raúl copies of my books. Raúl helped me contact participants for most of my studies in the past. When I entered the place, which was more affordable than Envy, I asked for Raúl. My friend who had visited that place took me to the dressing room where Raúl and some other gay guys were getting ready for the show. After saying hello to Raúl and giving him the books, I promised that I would stay to see his show. Lips had a different atmosphere than Envy. I saw couples dancing salsa, merengue, and Panama's folk music, "típico." I felt like I was back in time when if you were lucky, you could find your partner or next lover on the dance floor. I love salsa dancing and Panamanian folk music, so I asked my friend to dance with me and he pleased me. At midnight, Raúl came on stage dressed as a woman and sang two songs. After that, he introduced me to the audience as an LGBT writer and investigator living in the U.S. I felt like a celebrity that night. Then, he asked me to talk about my books and I did it. It was an amazing experience to be in that space where I felt that I belonged to and missed deeply.

Writing this book has not been easy since it is very close to my heart and my community. It was very hard for me to document and analyze my own anecdotes as a *maricón* and to connect them to the participants' experiences. However, I also experienced a sense of responsibility and empowerment while writing this book. Responsibility while using my privilege as an educated queer man in the U.S. to document the experiences of gay men in Panama, which is urgently needed in academia. I also felt empowered after listening to the participants' stories of pain and suffering. To answer the three research questions: How do self-identified gay men in Panama learn to navigate homophobia and other systems of oppression such as racism and classism? And what improvements have LGBT communities experienced in Panama? I developed four subheadings: Vulnerable Bodies, Gay Men Stereotypes, Trans Women's Journey, and *Maricón* Phobia.

1   Vulnerable Bodies

Raising a child requires a lot of work from responsible parents or caregivers. Recently, Panama's children's shelters were involved in an international scandal

(Noriega, 2021). It was denounced that orphan and/or abandoned children in some shelters were neglected and some of them were sexually assaulted by the adults who were supposed to take care of them. There were some protests on the streets and near the government headquarters that administers those shelters. However, like many other social issues in the country, some people were relocated from their jobs, while others were fired. The media did not continue covering this news and the children are still vulnerable to evil people. Being a child puts an infant in a vulnerable position; however, being an effeminate boy places a child in an even more vulnerable situation, especially if that boy does not get support from his parents, relatives, and teachers.

Effeminate boys are still bullied and oppressed at their schools, especially in public schools. A boy who chooses to be openly gay knows that he will be made fun of by other boys and sometimes teachers. Boys who start crossdressing as girls are not usually welcomed at schools. Instead, they are marginalized and oppressed. Most of them end up dropping out and start doing informal activities. In my interviews, I met some trans women who dropped out of school after receiving homophobic remarks from their parents, peers, and teachers (Ríos Vega, 2022). Other boys who realize that they like boys prefer to keep it a secret to avoid being rejected and/or punished by their parents and bullied or beaten up at school. A boy who does not follow gender expectations, especially in physical education, is targeted by their other male peers. Living in a patriarchal and machista society requires boys and men to perform their masculinity with very strict and tough patterns.

2 Gay Men Stereotypes

There is no doubt that social media has changed the way we socialize. When I used to live in Panama, the only way to socialize with other gay guys was to go out to gay clubs. After 22 years living in the United States things have changed drastically. Gay guys meet straight and gay men on apps such Grindr and Tinder. Gay clubs are no longer places where couples dance or single gay guys meet other guys. The drag shows start at midnight or later. Some gay clubs are more cliquish than others. The use of technology as a form of capitalism, reality shows from the United States, Mexico, Spain, and other South American countries, as well as the influx of immigrants, especially from Venezuela, Colombia, and Central America, have made the country more sexually diverse. I witnessed more guys identify as non-binary. During the Pride Month in June of 2022, I got involved in many panels and conferences. I was able to present

my book *Testimonios LGBTIQ+ in Panama*. In addition, I attended LGBT doc-
umentary presentations, art galleries, and walked the Pride March under the
rain.

Even though Panama seems to be more progressive than other countries
in the region, I realized that there are some issues that have not changed and
are usually taken for granted and/or internalized as a cultural issue instead of
naming it as a system of oppression. I was not surprised to hear some members of the LGBT community sharing homophobic incidents as normal. Unfortunately, when gay men end up internalizing those social expectations of what
society defines as being gay, they end up perpetuating those stereotypes, consciously and/or unconsciously. Gay men are found in all kinds of jobs and professions in Panama's society. Those who pass as straight and are middle class
might have more chances to be socially accepted. However, those who are
openly *maricones*, effeminate, Black, indigenous and/or belong to a low socioeconomic status, have more barriers to be part of the large society. Unfortunately,
in order to be socially accepted, the second group of gay men have no choice, but
to please society to be accepted even if it is just in specific spaces or queer spaces,
as I call them. For instance, there are two openly gay men who cross-dress as
women and who are very famous on TV. Both behave like stereotypical women,
those who like to gossip, to watch novelas, etc. As Ricardo Beteta, the president
of Hombres y Mujeres Nuevos de Panamá (AHMNP) mentioned, "as long as
the gay man is the joker, a clown or is made fun of, it is socially accepted. Once
the gay man critically analyzes oppression for being gay, people do not like us"
(R. Beteta, personal communication, September 27, 2018).

There are some queer spaces where gay men are accepted, similar to Beteta's
comments. Most people understand that gay men love beauty pageants, so
they use their talents to create amazing dresses for all kinds of queens, especially during the carnival season. Another stereotype is gay men's hairdressers
and fashionistas. I met some trans women who ended up working in beauty
salons as the only place where they were able to work dressed as women. Some
other stereotypical queer spaces represent folk singers such as Sammy y Sandra
Sandoval. Sandra has become an iconic figure in Panama, especially among gay
men since she usually sings songs that offend men or about love, revenge, and
womanhood. It is very common to see openly gay men, impersonators, and/or
drags dancing and/or moving their hips, emulating Sandra's exotic movements
on the stage. Another queer space, which I find contradictory, is in the Catholic
church. Some of my gay friends are in charge of decorating the saints with flow-
ers, ribbons, and more. I always find it bizarre that the catholic church is against
sex same marriage in Panama but allows gay men to decorate their saint altars.

FIGURE 1   Bernabé Ruíz Águila. Photo taken during the Gay Pride in Panama in 2011.
             This photo belongs to Bernabé Ruíz Águila

3   Trans Women's Journey

Over the years, some things in Panama have changed. For example, effeminate men, transvestites, and transsexuals can freely go out on the streets without fear of being arrested and imprisoned. The spaces for people of sexual diversity, such as discos and bars, ceased to be hidden and demonized places. Through dialogue and lobbying with the Electoral Court staff, more transgender people have been able to change their name on their ID without submitting medical tests that indicate a sex reassignment and avoid paying high costs to opportunistic lawyers. In addition, forming activists and pro-rights groups from diverse communities led by individuals of sexual diversity has created greater visibility in the general population, especially the media.

However, the lack of compliance with international laws signed by the different governments, and the constant interference of fundamentalist religious groups in the laws of the State, mean that the sexually diverse population continues to be vulnerable, marginalized, and, on many occasions, used as the object of ridicule. The heterosexual man who cross-dresses is always used as an object of fun and entertainment, especially in the media, since many times they obey a social pattern meant by being homosexual, a man who acts and wants to be a woman with highly exaggerated gestures. That does not mean that there are no homosexual men who cross-dress as women and call themselves drag queens and/or impersonators.

The question we ask ourselves is whether society, in general, knows how to differentiate the terms transvestite, transgender, transsexual, impersonator, and drag queen. We are sure of how the population still questions and rejects these vulnerable and defiant bodies before the patterns of what is "normal" and therefore accepted. All participants in this study reported having been victims of verbal and sometimes physical harassment by relatives and strangers due to their sexual orientation or gender expression. Some individuals even menace them with stones and sticks for the simple fact of wanting to be themselves.

Others have been used as objects of ridicule and insult in public spaces or seeking help in hospitals, police, and banks. They are called by their male names when going to medical appointments. A very recent case that drew worldwide attention during the COVID-19 pandemic was a gender and peak law implemented by Panama's government. This law gave specific days and hours for biological men and women to have access to leave their homes. This law revealed the marginality and invisibility of trans people in the country once again. When police officers and security guards saw these dissident bodies, whether as men or women, they were arrested, questioned, scolded, and even ridiculed. They were reminded they were not transgender people, but men dressed as women or women dressed as men. The police arrested them for not going out on the day that corresponded to them, according to their photo and sex documented on their identity cards. This event was a source of ridicule towards the trans population on different social networks. Through the pronouncement at the international level by even organizations pro-rights of trans people, the State sent a statement in this regard, but nothing was done. No one from the government apologized publicly.

Another significant challenge that trans people face is access to public education. Most of our participants shared how they were harassed and even ridiculed by their teachers and professors for not complying with masculine standards from very early on. Some were referred to psychologists or suspended from class for challenging homophobic comments from their teachers and classmates.

This lack of opportunities for education, classism, and institutionalized racism in Panama forces many the transvestites to engage in sex work. Others find acceptance in society as stylists in beauty salons or doing odd jobs. Nandin, Karla, and Sofía work as health promoters in a foundation for the rights of people of sexual diversity. They teach the population methods of preventing sexually transmitted diseases. We should remember that before being a health promoter, Karla was a sex worker on the streets.

We also know transvestites who have been raped in prison by their guards and forced to sign a document before leaving declaring that others did not violate their human rights. Likewise, hate crimes against the trans population have been reported. Still, in Panama, hate crimes against trans people are ignored and erased. The term hate crime does not exist under Panama's jurisdiction, giving homophobic and fundamentalist individuals free will to marginalize and oppress sexually diverse populations. It is essential to mention that Nandin and Sofia explained how omegids suffer many times more discrimination than other trans people for being Gunas.

Being part of the sexually diverse community in Panama has not been easy over the years. There is greater visibility today, but these dissident bodies are still vulnerable and oppressed through the hegemony of power perpetuated in the heteronormative educational system and a patriarchal society. Also, to conservative and fundamentalist religious ideologies, the media with homosexual characters and transvestites are stereotyped in State institutions, limiting their access to a better quality of life, education, and decent jobs.

4   *Maricón* Phobia

With the influence of reality shows from the United States, like Rupaul Race and streaming TV, young generations of LGBT individuals develop new gender identities that sometimes have no meaning in other spaces and societies. The use of English labels to sound trendy or the use of poor translations, without knowing the historical meaning of some terms in other contexts makes it more difficult to understand and/or to embrace a Panamanian LGBT identity. For example, while asking the participants in this study about the definition of the term gay, many of them defined it as liking somebody from the same sex or having sex with another man. What I found very interesting is how the use of an English term blurs diverse LGBT communities and how the use of the label can be used as a form of oppression to stereotype us. When I asked them about the use of Spanish words, such as *maricón, marica, cueco, pato,* ñaño,[1] most of them found those terms offensive. So, they preferred to use the English term gay.

The next question is whether the individual plays the binary role of active/active or if he identifies as versatile, which is a term that I hear constantly among young LGBT individuals. In addition to other new gender identities such as non-binary, pansexual, trans, and queer. What I find problematic with these new gender identities is how these dissident bodies are understood by mainstream society and how some of these new identities keep creating their own spaces to resist an oppressive and queerphobic society. Living in a homophobic society in Latin America is not as easy as some people might believe it is. Gay men, like the ones in this book, are still vulnerable due to multiple factors. Panama's education system is based on religious (Catholic beliefs), and most politicians are always afraid of losing votes during the elections if they advocate for LGBT rights. There is also a lack of critical education in LGBT communities that claims for social justice and human rights. Also, the use of English terms and gender identities makes it even more challenging for mainstream society to understand LGBT individuals. During my research studies, I learned how the terms gay, homophobia, transphobia, queer, transgender, transexual, and transvestite are still confusing to many LGBT individuals.

I call *maricón* phobia when people are afraid to talk about LGBT issues, especially in academia, or when self-identified LGBT individuals feel uncomfortable to engage in critical conversations about their own internalized homophobia and transphobia beyond binaries. In June 2022, I was invited to present my book in the Department of Sociology at the University of Panama, thanks to my colleague Luis Pulido Ritter.

Although I felt pleased with this presentation, I still find that Panama has a lot of work to do to create more spaces, especially in universities, public schools, and libraries where LGBT topics should be discussed through a critical lens. Besides presenting my book at the University of Panama, I was also able to visit the countryside (David), a well-known bookstore in the city, and attended some panels during Pride Month. I felt satisfied with my presentations and connections with other local leaders and younger LGBT communities. I was pleased to see a younger generation more interested in learning and unlearning about my writings, but I also realized that queerphobia still exists in Panama. I realized that some of the topics that I document in my writings as part of the LGBT history in Panama are still relevant today. Openly gay and effeminate men are still made fun of, oppressed, and marginalized, and trans women have fewer chances to complete their education due to a lack of acceptance and a more responsible curriculum that includes LGBT topics. Also, there is queerphobia within the LGBT community, especially when it intersects other social identities such as class and ethnicity. Afro-Panamanians and indigenous LGBT individuals experience more discrimination than white and mestizo gay men due to a Eurocentric definition of beauty and colorism (McGuinness, 2003).

5   LGBT Rights Are Human Rights

When I finally decided to write the conclusion of this book, I reflected on how things have changed in Panama since I felt it in 1999. On the surface, Panama has developed its infrastructure with skyscrapers, transnational company hubs, a modern metro system, and an international airport with better facilities. However, when you ask everyday Panamanians, you might realize that some things have not changed, especially when we talk about human rights for LGBT communities. Costa Rica (2020) and Colombia (2016), Panama's neighboring countries, approved same-sex marriage laws. Panama's government has attended international conferences, and congresses, and has compromised to follow international agreements about same-sex marriages; however, those promises are never crystalized. It is a clear example of how much influence the Catholic church and radical evangelical organizations have over the current governments and National Assembly politicians.

Since there are no specific laws to protect LGBT individuals and hate crimes do not appear as a specific form of crime, LGBT communities, especially trans women, are usually ignored and silenced by the Police Department and State. Panama's Police Department and Fire Department have specific regulations that do not allow openly LGBT individuals to be part of their institutions. Also, the Health Department does not accept blood donors who are part of the LGBT community. Public education is also another challenge for LGBT students. Students who behave out of their gender expectations are usually bullied by their peers and sometimes teachers and school administrators. Since these individuals are vulnerable in their own houses, especially if they come from low socioeconomic backgrounds, they have more chances to be oppressed in their schools, neighborhoods, and mainstream society. Trans women are usually pushed out of the school system once they start showing their femininity or cross-dressing. Most of these trans women have no choice but to become sex workers or to work in beauty salons. Araúz Reyes (2022) argues that,

> In Panama, there is no law that prohibits and sanctions the commission of discriminatory acts towards the LGBTIQ+ population, and this population is constantly subjected to verbal, psychological, patrimonial, economic, and physical violence by the social media, by the authorities— especially in the case of trans people—and the State itself, for its passivity and omission in the fulfillment of its duty as guarantor of the security of all the people who inhabit the country. (author's translation, p. 252)

As I mentioned earlier, the Catholic church has much influence on Panama's government. Whenever there is a social issue where the government and the protestors cannot come together, the government usually asks the Catholic church to become the intermediary, which I find very problematic since there is no separation between the church and the State in Panama. Although the Catholic church seems to be very anti-gay and homophobic, some priests, some of them well-known, have been involved in scandals related to hiring male sex workers or paying hotel rooms to men to hold parties (Cárdenas, 2019). In my research, I also discovered how some Catholic priests use their positions of power to seduce young boys who attend their churches. But there is something that I found interesting about the Catholic church and how it accepts openly gay men to decorate their Saints' altars during important holidays. I still do not understand this type of double standards between the Catholic church and openly gay men. It is like they are accepted in that specific space and moment when they are decorating the altars, but after that, they are no longer wanted.

With the help of the Internet, a new wave of immigrants, and collaboration with international human rights organizations and embassies, I noticed the awakening of pro-LGBT grassroots organizations and spaces. These organizations, usually led by LGBT-middle-class individuals, are educating their young LGBT population to have a better and more critical understanding of human rights, HIV/AIDS, mental health, self-care, and other relevant topics. In my last trip, I learned that young LGBT individuals are not afraid to express their sexuality in public and/or to create queer spaces where they can express themselves. However, I still fear that Panama does not have laws against homophobia and transphobia. I am concerned that my country has specific policies against LGBT individuals. LGBT teachers cannot talk openly about their sexuality, their partners, or their families, and that Panama does not have a same-sex marriage law that can protect those who decide to get married. It is not about getting married at a church or being dressed in a white bridal dress and black tuxedo, it is about protecting each other's wealth and making mutual decisions as a family. Panama has made some improvements, but there is still more to be done. As long as there are no human rights and legal rights laws that protect LGBT communities in the country, all of us will be *vulnerable bodies living on the edges.*

Note

1 Ñaño is an offensive term to refer to gay men in Panama.

Notes on Methods

In 2009, I decided to pursue my doctoral studies at The University of North Carolina at Greensboro. I must confess it was the first time I openly talked about my long-term relationships. It was also the first time that I experienced liberation and acceptance as a queer man of color in the United States. Thanks to my professor, I encountered a space where I could openly express my feelings and concerns about being queer and brown; however, I felt lonely since I was not able to connect with other Latinx queers in academia. I still recall how excited I felt when I read Arnaldo Cruz-Malavé's (2007) *Queer Latino Testimonio, Keith Haring, and Juanito Xtravanganza*. I also read *The Mariposa Boy* by Rigoberto González (2006). I talked to Dr. Bettez about my readings and how much I loved both books since the authors' stories sounded like my own writings. I then began attending conferences and realized that I was not alone anymore. I found amazing Latinx queers who inspired and continue inspiring my journey as a queer of color who loves to write. In 2011, I presented my first paper at a local conference where I reflected on my journey as a queer teacher in North Carolina. The following year, I published my first academic paper about being homosexual in Panama.

On one of my trips to my homeland, I decided to visit some local bookstores with the idea of finding some publications about homosexuality or LGBT studies in Panama. To my surprise my pursuit was unwelcome, and I received many frowned looks that made me feel like an outsider. I also visited the public libraries and my alma mater university library; however, I did not find any publication that would speak about the LGBT community from a social justice stance. I talked to some friends and colleagues and shared my concerns. Some of them agreed with my thoughts, while others did not find it necessary to document our experiences. I had mixed feelings about the situation and the lack of publications that focus on LGBT communities. I took it as a challenge and promised myself to start documenting these experiences. Since 2017, I have published two peer-reviewed articles, *An Unhealed Wound: Growing up Gay in Panama* (Ríos Vega, 2017a) and *Una Mariposa Transnacional Para Entender la Homosexualidad en Panamá* (2020), a book chapter, *When I Open My Alas: Developing a Transnational Mariposa Consciousness* (2019), and the book *Historias Desde el Sexilio* (2017) that narrates 10 fictional short stories that document purposeful themes within LGBT communities in Panama; *Carlos, the Fairy Boy* (2018) a children's book that explores gender construction in Panama through the eyes of a queer Latinx boy, and *Testimonios LGBTIQ+ de Panama* (2022). Writing and publishing about LGBT communities in Panama has not been an easy task since there is a form of internalized homophobia, sometimes, within LGBT individuals. Although I have published some of my research studies, it is my goal

© JUAN A. RÍOS VEGA, 2025 | DOI:10.1163/9789004714779_008

to allow an English-speaking audience to have an understanding of what it means to be a gay man within Panama's society. It is clear that there is not a single story about being LGBT; however, some of the narratives in this book share some commonalities. Unfortunately, some of the participants in this book still understand homophobia as the "norm" and being openly gay or trans as being "too much" or being "offensive" in regard to social norms. While these participants' stories tell us about the experience of being a gay man in Panama, all the participants are vulnerable bodies living on the edge of homophobia and sometimes dead.

Burton (2015) explains that in 1968, the Diagnostic and Statistical Manual of Mental Disorders (DSM)-II listed homosexuality as a mental disorder. However, in 1973, the American Psychiatric Association (APA) decided to remove it but replaced it with sexual orientation disturbance. It was not until 1987 that the DSM stopped referring to the term homosexuality as a mental disorder (when homosexuality stopped being a mental disorder). Panama's government finally eliminated the term homosexuality as an act of sodomy in 2008, becoming one of the last countries in the continent to do it. This date splits the documenting of the country's dissident bodies' history in a before and after. Panama's history revolves around colonization, like many other countries in the region, U.S. Imperialism, and the construction of the trans-isthmian railroad and The Panama Canal. All these historical events brought and keep bringing individuals from different venues and parts of the world. Its strategic geographical position has allowed people from all over to adopt the country as their new home. Panamanians have learned to live harmoniously with its indigenous groups, which were in the isthmus before the colonizers and other ethnic and racial groups.

Although interested individuals have dedicated their years to documenting social issues in Panama, there is almost no academic documentation that analyzes the experiences of gay men in the country. Since the term homosexuality has only recently been eliminated as a mental disease and the Catholic church has always considered homosexuality as a sin, there are no records that advocate for this marginalized group. Instead, local newspapers and religious leaders satanized those individuals who did not follow gender and social expectations. It is true that many things have changed since 2008; however, homophobia is so ingrained in Panama's society and everyday language that it is very challenging for mainstream, especially heterosexual individuals, to understand and unlearn their opinions about homophobia from this system of oppression. Additionally, some government offices, the police, and fire departments do not allow openly LGBT individuals. Some LGBT members must hide their sexual orientation due to fear of being rejected, oppressed, or fired. Panama's education system is another drawback since Catholicism is so embedded in the country's culture and the school curriculum. Talking about issues of sexuality and gender from a non-religious point of view is almost impossible due to these religious roots. This oppressive system allows teachers, administrators, and students to marginalize openly LGBT students, who are usually pushed out of the classrooms. Those who challenge the oppressive system have no choice but to conform to the homophobic system and hide their sexuality for many years or to accept it as the norm. Other LGBT individuals are disowned by their parents and decide to leave their houses, and some choose to live a double life (married men having sex with other men) to please social expectations.

1   From Colonialism to 21st Century Homosexuality in Panama:
       A Literature Review

Because we were not meant to survive, most jota/os have forged a unique spiritual maturity, one located on the margins of traditional institutions. This maturity has allowed us to focus our energies on fighting colonialism and oppression and to assemble an archive of healing spaces and practices that fulfill our spiritual needs (Calvo-Quiros, 2014, p. 192).

Before 1492, the Americas did not exist as a continent on any map because it had not been named at this time. The people who inhabited this part of the world named their own territories: Tawantinsuyu in Los Andes, Anahuac in what is today the Valley of Mexico, and Abya Yala in what Kuna Indians referred to today as Panama and Colombia. Mignolo (2005) claims that "People in Europe, in Asia, and in Africa had no idea of the landmass soon to be called the Indias Occidentales and then America" (p. 2). Throughout history, traditional studies have interpreted indigenous groups and ways of life from a colonizing lens, making them out to be primitive, inferior, and unintelligent. For many postcolonial scholars of color (Banales, 2014; Coloma, 2013; Cruz, 2012; Hames-Garcia, 2014a; Hames-Garcia & Martinez, 2011; Ocampo, 2012; Perez, 2014; Rodriguez, 2003; Tijerina Revilla & Santillana, 2014; Thuiwai Smith, 2002; Urrieta, 2003), claims are made for the interpretation of indigenous and marginalized groups from a non-traditional lens as an urgent and critical space in academia. Tuhiwai Smith (2002) argues that "under colonialism, indigenous peoples have struggled against a Western view of history and yet been complicit with that view. We have often allowed our 'histories' to be told and have then become outsiders in this process" (p. 33).

Although few research studies have been developed in Central America and the Caribbean about sexual practices during the pre-colonial period, some have revealed a different definition of sexuality than what it is today. Chronicles written in XV, XVI, and XVII mentioned different types of homosexuality as a common form of sexuality before Europeans called it sodomy (translated Diversidad sexual en Abya Yala). Sigal (2003) quoted,

> When the Spaniards and Portuguese wrote about the conquest of Latin America, they used many descriptions to denigrate the indigenous populations. Probably

the three most common and, to Europeans, most extraordinary images in these chronicles of the conquest were human sacrifice, cannibalism, and sodomy. (p. 1)

Europeans used their homophobic and racist beliefs to convince indigenous peoples that the reason for their diseases and floods was god's punishment for them for having same-sex relationships. Trexler (1995) argues that sodomy or male homosexuality allowed Europeans to conquer, proclaiming to indigenous people that sodomy was their downfall. For that reason, "the wrathful Christian god had decided to send the Iberians to conquer the Americas because they had engaged in homosexual behavior" (p. 84).

The most atrocious example of the European conquest, especially what they called an act of sodomy and the first account of homosexuality in the American continent, occurred during Balboa's trek across the Isthmus of Panama. After Alvarez Chanca's mere hint of a military berdache in his letter of 1494, the American domestic berdache appears clearly for the first time in the accounts of Balboa's discovery of the Pacific in 1513. In the third decade of his De orbe novo, published in 1516, the Italian Peter Martyr d'Anghiera tells how, in his trek across Panama, Balboa found a brother of the cacique of Quaraca and some of his men dressed as women and practicing sodomy (nefanda ... Venere). The conquistador quickly threw some forty of these transvestites (though apparently not their active partners!) to the dogs, the first record of Spanish punishment of sodomy on the American continent. According to Peter Martyr, it all happened to the applause of the native subjects, 'for the contagion was confined to the courtiers and had not yet spread to the people' (Trexler, 1995, p. 82).

Although Trexler's studies on gender before and during the Spanish and Portuguese period, his Westernized definition while referring to non-traditional gendered men as "berdache," perpetuates the idea of negative gender performance, which was totally accepted by indigenous groups before colonization.

Balboa and his people used Christianity to convince people that they were living in sin and that their god had sent them to save the native people; however, they also constructed a gender-role performance and convinced indigenous peoples that sodomy or homosexuality was contagious. Balboa and other Spaniards sent the message that they would not tolerate any type of non-traditional sexual act (man and woman), including men dressing as women and/or performing women's roles (Sigal, 2003).

Amazingly, this negative and sometimes sinful idea of seeing men dressed as women or effeminate men has dominated our Latin American societies for centuries. In Panama, for example, the catholic church and the government have influenced society, especially by promoting homosexuality as a threat against mankind. This way of thinking has pushed homosexual men and women to abandon their families, hide their sexual orientation, or live a double life (marrying someone of the opposite gender to please their families and society while still having the same sex as someone of the same gender).

Javier Stanziola (2013a, 2013b), who has won multiple writing contests in Panama on homosexuality topics in the isthmus and abroad, shares that Panama, like most Latin American countries, rules that same-sex couples cannot get married and/or adopt children. As a result, homosexuals have no choice but to abandon their country to look for this type of freedom. He says, "The only choice is to immigrate and reinvent ourselves in places where our Panamanian identities become stereotyped or lumped as a single and static group: either in Europe or a rural town in the United States" (p. 16). Unfortunately, although parents and families are aware of their family member or friend who happens to be homosexual, they prefer to avoid talking about it as if it does not exist. They still internalize homosexuality as a sinful and shameful behavior. Some others believe that young people usually engage in homosexual behaviors but will eventually change due to age, maturity, or religion.

2   U.S. Imperialism

This idea of understanding homosexuality as an act of sodomy has not changed that much throughout the years in most Latin American countries due to double-standard societies and religious beliefs imposed through colonization. However, it did not stop people from creating a homosexual subculture in the isthmus. For instance, due to the presence of the U.S. American bases in the isthmus, there exist some archives of a homosexual subculture in Panama (1903–1999) in an area known as the Canal Zone, where locals were not allowed to enter. This area became a perfect space for prostitution and homosexuality to be exercised. Donoghue (2014) argues:

> U.S. efforts at enforcing sexual controls at the borders "provided a key site for the production and reproduction of sexual categories, identities, and norms" among the typically unequal relations that abounded along an imperial frontier. For example, Canal Zone Police and MPs frequently arrested sexual transgressors" along the enclave's borders and categorized, classified, and ascribed behaviors and identities to them that were often untrue, mistaken, or self-serving for the U.S. border-control mission. Thus, Panamanian lovers became prostitutes; effeminate Colombian males homosexuals; and Panamanian Carnaval revelers cross-dressers. (p. 131)

It was common knowledge to hear people talking about U.S. soldiers having sex with men dressed as women and/or prostitutes, who used to wait for U.S. soldiers, mainly as they exited the Canal Zone areas or the U.S. American bases during the night. La 4 de Julio (July 4th) was a well-known street where most homosexuals and prostitutes used to wait for their U.S. soldier sexual encounters. Donoghue (2014) quotes: "In some cases, U.S. soldiers reported that they had been raped in the republic by Panamanian males" (p. 158). However, officials were always doubtful about U.S. soldiers' excuses for having anal bleeding or venereal diseases since previous incidents indicated how homosexual practices and/or same-sex sexual encounters took place within the U.S. American bases.

3   Militarism

But even while Noriega's power was growing, the bisexual side of his personality began to emerge more openly, still concealed by the macho image he was carefully cultivating. The macho officer, proficient in judo and parachuting, would perfume himself heavily on off-hours and wear yellow jumpsuits with yellow shoes, would travel the world with a pilot boyfriend, with whom he was widely rumored to be having a torrid affair, and would surround himself with openly gay ambassadors and personal advisors (Kempe, 1990, p. 83).

Another dark period in Panama occurred during our military regimes (1968–1989), especially against those who opposed oppression and persecution. Politicians and civilians who tried to resist Noreiga, including homosexuals, were victims of persecution, oppression, incarceration, verbal and physical abuse, and even rape. Koster and Sanchez (1990) narrate how Dr. Ricardo Arias Calderon, an outstanding philosopher and Panamanian politician, was arrested on June 9, 1987, after some protests against Noriega's dictatorship.

> Later, in the G-2 courtyard, Ricardo and the others he was with were made to lie face down on the ground and were threatened with rape and had condoms held in front of them and were told they'd be put in La Modelo and raped by prisoners, most of whom had AIDS. (p. 334)

I still recall how as a teenager, my older relatives used to talk about these rumors of politicians who opposed Noriega's regime being raped in jail. Some others used it as a joke to threaten civilians as to what might happen to them if they broke the law. Another example involving homosexuality and abusive behavior occurred in a very infamous jail in Panama City known as La Preventiva. It was a very seedy, hot, and small place where most men were taken after being arrested. La Preventiva was also a place where homosexuals were raped by other prisoners, usually criminals and sometimes police officers.

Sometime after midnight, the sergeant in jeans came in with marijuana cigarettes for the criminals who'd been working as harassers. The smokes calmed them down, but then a young woman was thrust inside, what looked like a young woman to the politicals, in high heels and pedal pushers and a pink blouse. Actually, it was a male transvestite. And frequent visitor at La Modelo evidently, for the criminals greeted him by name, by nom de guerre, Carolina. With great enthusiasm, the reason for which was immediately evident, for (following what seemed an established pecking order) they at once began to make sexual use of him. With his consent first, or at least resignation, and then despite his pleas and protests, his whimpering and tears—twenty or more acts of oral and anal intercourse, with wisecrack accompaniment from those who'd already coupled or were waiting their turns and cuffs, ear twistings, and curses to encourage Carolina (p. 346).

This constant abusive behavior was sometimes staged in front of arrested politicians as a threat to what might happen to them later. The fact that homosexuals were sexually abused and sometimes raped while in jail was commonly seen as their own fault for being open homosexuals. A good example of how openly gay men were targeted in Panama is portrayed in the play *La Madrid*, written by Pablo Salas (2005), a well-known local scriptwriter and actor:

Ezequiel:

Por la hijueputa salazón que cargo, me pillaron escribiendo con pintura de spray, "Noriega Maricón" ... Cono, me puse del mismo color de la pintura ... blanca!

For being son of a bitch I have bad luck. They (police) caught me writing with spray, Noriega faggot ... Damn, I turned the same color as the paint ... white!

Anel:

Y entonces?

And then?

Ezequiel:

Lo bueno fue que el tongo que me agarro era como medio gay. Tu sabes que lo primero es dar de toletazos y luego preguntan. Este me trato como una princesa. Me mandarin para el cuartel de Tinajitas y me encerraron con unos chombones de alta peligrosidad, dizque para que mi noche fuera tortuosa.

The good thing is that the guy that arrested me was like gay. You know, first they beat you with a stick and then they ask questions. This one treated me like a princess. I was sent to Tinajitas (a prison) and locked me up with "chombones" (strong

*black men), so I could have a pleasant night (meaning prisoners might have sex
with or rape him).*

La Madrid was like a borderland, bringing clients from all different social backgrounds and experiences. It was a small, smelly, and seedy bar in Casco Viejo in
Panama City where homosexuals, intellectuals, prostitutes, and even thieves shared
their life experiences, where nobody was asked or questioned. It represented a risk-
free space for individuals who looked for a neutral place to challenge social norms and
religious beliefs. Ezquiel's story with the police was not new to many homosexuals
who, like me, used to visit La Madrid to meet old and new friends.

4   21st Century

Homosexuality has always been a taboo topic in society, and it has pushed homosexuality and same-sex encounters to become a secret behavior and/or act. Homosexuality
is still punishable and seen as an immoral act in society. For example, homosexuals are
not allowed to have access to certain human rights, cannot find decent jobs, and are
sometimes marginalized by families and society at large. In the case of the National
Police Department, gays and lesbians are not allowed. Instead, they are considered as
somebody who is dangerous toward others, aggressive, unintelligent, an alcohol addict,
and/or a physical abuser. On the other side, there have been some reports where police
officers become verbally and physically abusive toward transsexuals and homosexuals.
Homosexuals are victims of sexual assaults and violent and aggressive treatment, and
some have been asked to pay illegal fees to police officers (R. Beteta, personal communication, September 27, 2018).

The local media also discriminates against homosexuals and lesbians with derogatory and discriminatory arguments, perpetuating the double-standard society of a
homosexual who is rejected by society for breaking institutionalized binaries. At the
same time, a homosexual is accepted if he fits the mold of being effeminate and/or is a
hair stylist, fashion designer, and loves beauty pageants and carnival queens or someone who keeps his/her sexual orientation as something private even when everybody
else realizes the individual's sexual orientation. In a recent study, Castillero (2012) found
that in Panama the gay, lesbian, bisexual, and transgender (GLBT) group still experiences positive and negative issues. For instance, on the negative side, self-identified
GLBT individuals find a lack of representation and equality in professions such as police
officers, engineers, and architects. Self-identified GLBT, in this case, men who happen
to have sex with other men are not allowed to be blood donors. In addition, the word
"gay" cannot be used to advertise or to market businesses in Panama since it contradicts
Panamanians' moral values. According to Araúz Reyes (2022):

At no time in the history of Panama has the LGBTIQ+ population been included in national censuses or in public registries of this or any other nature to determine demographic aspects such as age, sex and place of residence of this population, as well as as to determine the social characteristics such as occupation, family situation or income of the LGBTIQ+ population, to know their needs and, from the State, establish affirmative policies with a view to equity and equality. The above, despite the fact that in recent years there have been requests from LGBTIQ+ groups in this regard, as well as recommendations from international organizations and even other States, through the Universal Periodic Reviews. (author's translation, p. 249)

On the positive side, since April 2002, by law the Republic of Panama grants protection to individuals who have been discriminated against due to their sexual orientation. In addition, since 2006, the Dirección General de Cedulación del Tribunal Electoral (Vital Records Office) allows a legal attorney to help an individual's claim to change his/her sex on his/her birth certificate based on the individual's gender self-identification. Finally, Executive Law #332, as of July 29, 2008, eliminated Article 12 of Law 149 from May 20, 1949, that penalized sodomy (a word used to name homosexuality before 1973). (translated). Although things seem to change for the better in Panamanian society toward a more inclusive LGBT group, there are still some institutionalized norms and regulations based on religious beliefs, a double-standard society, and political agendas that hinder the creation of a State law that protects and grants legal rights to the LGBT group. Araúz Reyes (2022) posits that

LGBTIQ+ people in Panama do not have protection against discrimination either at the legislative level or in terms of public policies, in turn having lack of protection in all areas of life in society: civil, labor, educational, political, economic and social. (p. 244)

5   Methodology

As a scholar, I experienced some frustration for not finding a voice within queer studies, a voice that could speak about the homosexual experience of Latino males, especially in Panama. Reading Hames-Garcia's and Martínez's (2011) article titled *Queer Theory Revisited* allowed me to find a niche in traditional queer studies. I learned that I was not alone in my quest to address Latino/a queerness from a non-traditional ontology. For example, Hames-Garcia and Martínez (2011) posit that even though white queers have been using "theories of color," these theories have only been used as part of their footnotes to support their claims (p. 26). He argues that queer theory and lesbian and gay studies have not been able to address "theories of color" correctly; they have only become part of queer genealogies for strategic purposes. Hames-Garcia and Martínez (2011) argue that race, gender, sexuality, and class are constantly interrelated and not occasionally intersected like other scholars have theorized. He claims that queer theory lacks an analysis of race and its interrelations with other identities (p. 29). Kumashiro (2001) agrees stating that an identity only has meaning when it is related to other identities; there can never be an identity that is all-inclusive (p. 6). Hames-Garcia and Martínez (2011) claim that "the contributions of people of color are necessary since they can provide a look into how their topics relate to race and how race is interrelated to other identities" (p. 29).

The lack of relevant analysis on queers of color and in-depth discussions of race, gender, and sexuality, led to a new split within queer studies called "queer of color critique." Drawing from women of color, feminism, lesbian feminism, transformational feminisms, radical philosophies, U.S. Third World feminism, and anticolonial theorists, queer of color critique develops a better understanding of how race, sexuality, gender, and other forms of oppression are interrelated. Queer and non-queer scholars challenge dominant (White) epistemologies in order to analyze oppression and the marginalization of people of color, especially queers of color, by sharing their own histories, counter narratives, and *testimonios* while giving birth to new epistemologies. Some scholars of color have decided to expand on gay, lesbian, and queer studies to raise their voices in academia while others have decided to move away from a queer identity. "A queer of color critique" has dismantled and continues dismantling how queer sexualities were normalized in places like Africa, South Asia, and Latin America and how queer sexualities have persisted despite U.S. colonialist practices (Kumashiro, 2001, p. 7). To analyze how those queer sexualities were normalized as a result of colonialism, queer scholars have drawn a line and called it "colonial difference" and "modern sexuality" (Hames-Garcia & Martínez, 2011, p. 40).

Within that "colonial difference" approach, scholars have unveiled how some "native cultures" traditionally viewed gender and sexuality in very different ways than the binary system that predominates Euro-American thought: a system that stipulates that we are male or female, masculine or feminine, straight, or gay (Kumashiro, 2001, p. 7). As a result, queers of color scholars have invested their time to understand how queers of color have resisted oppression and marginalization as part of colonization, immigration, slavery, capitalism, and post-colonialism. Stavans (1996) argues that homosexuals represent

> the other side of Hispanic sexuality, a shadow one refuses to acknowledge—
> a "they" that is really an "us." Again, the language betrays us: the panoptic array of
> terms for homosexual include *alabado, adelito, afeminado, ahembrado, amaricado,*
> *amujerado, barbalindo, carininfo, cazolero, cocinilla, enerve, gay, homosexual, inver-*

tido, lindo, maría, marica, mariposa, ninfo, pisaverde, puto, repipí, sodomita, volteado, zape, to name only a few. (p. 155)

6   Autoethnography

> Our transnational autoethnographies aim to decenter mainstream U.S.-American approaches to autoethnography. We are critical because we know that now, our voices matter, and we can tell powerful stories with words that might need translations. After all, we all cross borders. (Atay, 2021, p. 301)

I have always been an autoethnographer, a storyteller even before understanding it as an academic term. I always liked to make connections with my readings, readings that speak about me and my communities. Finding books that speak about Latinx LGBT communities within the U.S. and overseas was not easy at the beginning. Due to my lack of knowledge, I always thought that scholars did not include LGBT topics in their studies or Latinx LGBT communities were too busy dealing with other social issues like racism and classism to write about issues of same-sex attraction. I still recall when I found the book *Queer Latino Testimonio,* by Keith Harding, and *Juanito Xtravaganza* by Armando Cruz-Malavé (2007). I read this book with so much joy. I found this book as a sign of hope and home. Then when I was in my doctoral program, I shared this book with Dr. Bettez as I had found a treasure. Afterward, I found the book that inspired me to write my own biography. Rigoberto González's (2006) *Butterfly Boy: Memories of a Chicano Mariposa,* gave me the wings to take off. I realized that Rigoberto's stories were very similar to mine. I discovered that his anecdotes about being a gay boy intersected with my experiences even though we belong to two different generations and places. However, I still missed the fact that I could not find stories that spoke about the Central American or Caribbean experiences of gay or queer boys and men. I do not remember how I read Reinaldo Arenas's (1993) book *Before Night Falls.* His story about being a dissident writer in Cuba and then moving to the United States allowed me to make strong connections with his experiences as a Cuban and gay immigrant. His memories from his homeland, what it meant to be gay in machista Latin American and Caribbean countries became music to my ears. Today, I can honestly attest that Armando Crúz-Malavé, Rigoberto González, and Reinaldo Arenas gave me the strength and the empowerment to document my personal experiences as a queer of color and *maricón* with others. Chang (2008) states that

> Autoethnographers attempt to achieve cultural understanding through analysis and interpretation. In other words, autoethnography is not about focusing on self alone, but about searching for an understanding of others (culture/society) through self. (p. 49)

This constant personal reflection about my sexual identities inspired me to write about my own experiences as a queer of color while finding connections with other LGBT individuals with similar experiences, experiences that are rarely found in textbooks (Chang, 2008; Chang et al., 2013; Poulos, 2021). "Autoethnographic researchers can tap into their most personal thoughts and experiences that are not readily opened to others" (Chang et al., 2013, p. 21).

Using autoethnography as a qualitative method in this book also allows me to examine my own experiences as a transnational mariposa who is in constant movement, traveling between two geographical spaces, which make me more reflexive about my binary identities (queer of color/*maricón*). In Adams and Holman Jones (2011), Madison (1998) claims that

> Autoethnography, queer theory, and reflexivity share commitments that are personal and political, tense and complicated, disruptive and open-to-revision, humane, and ethical … such interrogation involves a rigorous call for reflexivity— to reflect not only on the self, how the self works, and how others are implicated by the self and the self's desires, but also on how we represent—in writing, performance, film, and so on—the process and challenges of reflection. (p. 111)

This constant traveling pushes me to become more careful about how I perceive myself in different spaces, but it also allows me to step back and analyze LGBT individuals in a deeper and more reflective manner. Saldaña and Omasta (2018) claim that "Ethnography is the introspective examination of one's culture through a "culture-of-one's experiences" (p. 158). Being able to reconnect and to listen to my LGBT community in Panama and to reflect on my own experiences as a queer of color in the United States gives me the opportunity to analyze what it means to be gay/queer/maricón in two different geographical spaces. It allows me to analyze how things have and have not changed in my homeland since I left it in 1999. Poulos (2021) posits that "Autoethnographers actively engage researcher reflexivity, grounded in systematic introspection, bringing personal insight to the project of ethnographic research" (p. 16). This exercise also reminds me that LGBT individuals make sense of their own surroundings, which means that my reflexivity also tells me that I must be very careful about my comments since I no longer live in Panama and that my privileges as a transnational citizen can be misinterpreted by my community. Chang (2008) points out that writing ethnography has many benefits since it allows the researcher to engage in self-reflection that can lead to "self-transformation through self-understanding." This leads the researcher to develop a "cultural understanding of self and the potential of cross-cultural coalition building with others" (p. 57). Adams and Holman Jones (2011) claim that "Reflexive means listening to and for the silences and stories we can't tell— not fully, not clearly, not yet; returning, again and again, to the river of story accepting what you can never fully, never unquestionably know" (pp. 111–112).

As a transnational mariposa and autoethnographer from Panama who can easily cross linguist borders, I can reach out to my community in Spanish (although my mother tongue no longer sounds like mainstream Panamanians due to the extensive use of the English language). Sharing anecdotes and making connections with my peers, especially those who share the same age and who visited the same gay clubs, bars, and LGBT events that I did while living or visiting Panama allowed me to develop a sense of trust and a permanent connection. As an autoethnographer, I use my personal experiences as primary data to explore and critique the experiences of gay men in Panama (Chang, 2008; Holman Jones et al., 2013)

These experiences of being an insider and outsider within my own community have given me the opportunity to be an active participant in multiple events. As an insider, I always visit Panama June-July to participate and collaborate during Pride month. I have been invited to give lectures, workshops, and panels about my LGBT studies. I donate funds to support LGBT organizations, and I always walk along with my community during the Pride annual march. As an outsider, besides writing academic documents about my community, I also use my research to write fictional texts (short stories, poems, plays, film scripts, and a novel) since I want more audiences besides academia to learn about my community. According to Holman Jones et al. (2013), "Autoethnographers strive to write accessible prose that is read by a general audience, but they also try to construct the work so it steps into the flow of discussion around a topic of interest to researchers" (p. 23). Poulos (2021) claims that "Autoethnographers write to discover, inquire, explore, and show rather than tell a reader what is known ... autoethnographers use writing to learn about ourselves, our social worlds, our communicative acts, and our social engagements" (p. 17).

To give the readers of this book a deeper understanding of my ethnographic book, I use Holman Jones et al.'s (2013) purposes of autoethnography outlines and align them with my book.

6.1   *Disrupting Norms of Research Practice and Representation*

Since autoethnographers use their personal experiences as the core data, I found it important to use my dual identities as a queer of color in the United States and *maricón* in Panama to connect and document my experiences and the experiences of the LGBT community in my homeland. It is through those conversations formally and informally with my friends and colleagues that I feel empowered to document my personal narratives and peers' experiences while navigating Panama's society. Adams and Holman Jones (2011) claim that

> The autoethnographic means that sharing politicized, practical, and cultural stories that resonate with others and motivating these others to share theirs; bearing witness, together, to possibilities wrought in telling. (p. 111)

It is my role as an academic and autoethnographer, living in the United States and able to communicate in two languages that I am able to listen, translate, and document my LGBT community. It is this privilege that allows me to bring a different experience of being a translational gay/*maricón* researcher and scholar to expand the studies about LGBT individuals in Latin American countries, especially in Central America. Finally, it is my intentionality to purposefully reappropriated the offensive and homophobic term *maricón*, as a form of rebellion and empowerment, to talk about my lived experiences as gay man in Panama and my transnational mariposa consciousness as queer of color in the United States to document the experiences LGBT individuals in my homeland.

6.2   *Working from Insider Knowledge*

As a self-identified *maricón* and well-known in the LGBT community in Panama, besides my active participation during Pride month and sponsor of LGBT organizations, I am constantly working from my inside knowledge. When I am not in Panama, I am still in touch with LGBT leaders and community members through social media. "Working from insider knowledge, autoethnographers use personal experience in order to facilitate understanding of those experiences" (Geertz, 1973, p. 33). I keep collecting information (pictures, newspapers, videos, and other forms of artifacts) that can help me with my writings about my community. Atay (2021) argues that "Autoethnography as a method aims to empower scholars by allowing them to narrate their stories and experiences within a culture as they experience it" (p. 296).

Additionally, I share my studies and publications with my community and other interested individuals whenever I visit my homeland. My previous publications (especially in Spanish) are used by my college and other researchers within Panama and Latin America.

6.3   *Maneuvering through Pain, Confusion, Anger, and Uncertainty and Making Life Better*

This book is the result of my constant drafting and writing every time I visited my homeland and met my old friends and colleagues. I became very reflective about my community. I felt anger and still feel it when I realize that many things have not changed after over 20 years. It is true that LGBT individuals from younger generations are more visible, brave, and outspoken; however, their State has not passed laws to protect LGBT individuals, especially trans women and men, and same-sex marriage. There is no law that typifies the killing of LGBT individuals as a hate crime. These issues make me realize how vulnerable LGBT people still are in my homeland. Burke (1974) says:

> In autoethnography we see an explicit and intentional directedness toward others, either through the offering of insight that might help those who relate to a

person's experience or in a desire for others to bear witness to particular struggles. By processing painful, confusing, angering, and uncertain cultural experiences, the autoethnographer can make life better by giving others "equipment for living." (p. 35)

This is why I decided to write this book. I want researchers, college students, and other interested individuals beyond Panama's borders to have a deeper understanding of the struggles within my community. I want to use my privilege as an educated person who can document and publish this type of information to echo my personal experiences and the experiences of LGBT individuals in Panama.

6.4   *Breaking Silence/(re)Claiming Voice and "Writing to Right"*

Being openly gay/*maricón* or trans in Panama is not easy at all. Individuals navigate society living on the edges of vulnerability, sometimes risking their own lives. These individuals do not usually trust the authorities (police department), religious leaders, and teachers. Some of them are disowned by their parents and oppressed by relatives, friends, and society in general. There is a need to document my community. Although there is more access to LGBT literature in Spanish and English in Panama, there is a lack of academic literature that documents the experiences of LGBT in Panama from a social justice lens and written by someone who belongs to that community. Despite contingencies and difficulties of writing toward and for liberation, some autoethnographers use personal experiences to describe cultural experiences and to go "against the current social order" (DeLeon, 2010, p. 409).

6.5   *Making Work Accessible*

I am not only a queer color scholar, but a fictional writer, scriptwriter, poet, and also puppeteer. Purposefully, during the pandemic, I took writing workshops online from State agencies in Panama. I used those spaces for two reasons: to learn how to become a better novel, script, and poem writer and to disrupt "the norm" (heteronormativity, racism, and misogyny). I wanted to use part of my personal experiences as a *maricón* and the voices of other LGBT individuals to echo our experiences in machista spaces. Adams and Holman Jones (2011) claim,

> Autoethnography—a method that uses personal experience with a culture and/ or cultural identity to make unfamiliar characteristics of the culture and/or identity familiar for insiders and outsiders–and queer theory—a dynamic and shifting theoretical paradigm that developed in response to a normalizing of heterosexuality and from a desire to disrupt insidious social conventions—share cooperative ideological commitments. (p. 110)

I know that my writings made some people feel uncomfortable, but it was all intentional. I wanted my peers to have a clear understanding of my community's experiences. I also wanted some individuals to understand that sometimes, their writings about my community are based on prejudgments and stereotypes about my community.

> Han pasado dos generaciones ya desde que el maricón dejó su tierra natal. Su amor por otros maricones y mariconas se demuestra en sus escritos y en su conexión con otras locas, cuecos, cuecas, lesbianas, maricones, trans y tortilleras.

> Two generations have passed since the maricón left his homeland. His love for other maricones and mariconas is demonstrated in her writings and in his connection with other locas, cuecos, cuecas, lesbians, maricones, trans and tortilleras. (Ríos Vega, 2022, p. 203)

All of these online courses allowed me to raise my voice and the voices of my community. I created short stories, poems, and scripts, and as I am writing this book, I am also working on my first novel in Spanish. In addition, I met a local and young queer film director in Panama, so we submitted a film proposal for an annual film contest in Panama. Hopefully, I will be able to produce a different form of literature (visual) to echo the experiences of trans women during COVID-19 in Panama. Amaral Palevi Gómez (2016) in his essay *Travestis, marimachas y maricones: el camino del arcoiris en El Salvador* claims that

> The invisibility of these entities has possibly been the unspoken rule for not giving attention to LGBT people. When such identities are visible, attempts are made to deny them their rights, as in the case of the legalization of their associations and organizations in the corresponding State agencies. (p. 109)

It is through my writings and publications that I want to bring awareness about the LGBT culture and community in Panama. It is through my literature that I want to echo my experiences and the experiences of LGBT individuals. As a queer/*maricón* storyteller, it is my hope that my book can help others to get access to real and clear knowledge about this oppressed community. It is not easy to be openly LGBT in many countries around the world. As I mentioned previously, it is my goal that this book can also be a resource in the field of education. Developing a transnational consciousness to theorize and analyze my experiences as a queer of color in the United States and *maricón* in a Latin American country will serve as a springboard for pre-service and in-service teachers, as well as instructors in the school of education to have a deeper understanding about the everyday experiences of LGBT communities outside of the United States. It will also allow interested readers to find relevant literature in English that voices the experiences of marginalized communities in a Central American country.

There is still a lot of injustice institutionalized by governments and perpetuated by institutions and ignorant individuals. When there are no laws specifically created to protect marginalized communities like my LGTB community in Panama, our bodies become vulnerable every single day that we step out into the world. Younger generations can claim that things are better now than 20 or 30 years ago, and that might be true; there is more visibility and people are more educated about their human rights. Some non-profit LGBT organizations are advocating and claiming their rights; however, in the meantime, our bodies and lives as *maricones, mariconas, marimachas,* trans, travestis, *cuecas, cuecos, patos,* ñaños, queers, gays are still living on the edges of injustice, violence, and death. "Panama sells an image internationally that does not match the national reality. There is no agreement between what is said and done, we want things to improve, but we resist changes; This is a serious contradiction" (Beteta Bond, 2022).

7   Ethical Concerns

I carefully studied the research ethics for this study. I clearly shared with my participants that I had permission from my university to develop this study. I showed them the approved research proposal and informed consent forms. While explaining the informed consent form to the participants, I let them know that their names would be changed to protect their narratives as gay men in Panama. I shared with them that the recorded interviews would be locked in file cabinets and that I was the only person with access to those interviews. I also shared that I would personally translate the interviews into English. I am convinced that my honest conversations and sense of trust with the participants allowed them to share personal information about their experiences as LGBT in Panama.

References

Adams, T. E. (2021). On (not) living past 30. In E. Rodríguez-Doranz (Ed.), *The everyday lives of gay men* (pp. 58–68). Routledge.

Adams, T. E., & Holman Jones, S. (2011). Telling stories: Reflexivity, queer theory, and autoethnography. *Cultural Studies <=> Critical Methodologies*, 11(2), 108–116.

Anzaldúa, G. (2007). *Borderlands/La Frontera: The new mestiza* (3rd ed.). Aunt Lute Books.

Araúz Reyes, N. M. (2022). Un bicentenario de exclusión: Situación jurídica de las minorías sexuales en Panamá. In A. Arévalo, D. Arrocha, J. Ríos-Vega, & L. Herra (Eds.), *Alternaridades sexuales centroamericanas en el bicentenario* (pp. 230–260). Clacso.

Arenas, R. (1993). *Before night falls*. Penguin Group.

Atay, A. (2021). Translation and tango: Decolonizing autoethnography. In T. A. Adams, S. Holman, & C. Ellis (Eds.), *Handbook of autoethnography* (2nd ed., pp. 295–302). Routledge.

Banales, X. (2014). Joteria: A decolonizing political project. *Aztlan: A Journal of Chicano Studies*, 39(2), 155–165.

Baños, O. (2020). *Las luciérnagas quizá no volverán*. Los Ángeles, California: Library of Congress Catalog Card.

Beteta Bond, R. (2022). Existimos y resistimos: La lucha de los panameños LGBTIQ+. *La Prensa*. 9 de diciembre del 2022.

Britton, R. M. (1999). *Teatro*. Litho Editorial.

Britton, R. M. (2002). *Laberintos de orgullo*. Santillana, S.A.

Burke, K. (1974). *The philosophy of literary form: Studies in symbolic action* (3rd ed.). University of California Press.

Burton, N. (2015, September 15). *When homosexuality stopped being a mental disorder*. https://www.psychologytoday.com/us/blog/hide-and-seek/201509/when-homosexuality-stopped-being-a-mental-disorder

Calvo-Quiroz, W. A. (2014). The aesthetics of healing and love: An epistemic genealogy of jota/o aesthetic traditions. *Aztlan: A Journal of Chicano Studies*, 39(1), 181–194.

Cantú, L. (2009). *The sexuality of migration: Border crossings and Mexican immigrant men*. New York University Press.

Cárdenas, H. (2019, December 6). *El sacerdote David Cosca continúa suspendido por la Iglesia; confirma la Arquidiócesis*. https://www.prensa.com/judiciales/el-sacerdote-david-cosca-continua-suspendido-por-la-iglesia-confirma-la-arquidiocesis/

Castillero, C. J. (2012). *Informe nacional sobre la situación de los derechos humanos de la poblacion gay, lesbiana, bisexual, y transexual (GLBT) de la Republica de Panama* (Junio 2011-Junio 2012).

Chang, H. (2008). *Autoethnography as method*. Left Coast Press.

Chang, H., Wambura Ngunjiri, F., & Hernandez, K. C. (2013). *Collaborative autoethnography*. Left Coast Press.

Coloma, R. S. (2013). Ladlad and parrhesiastic pedagogy: Unfurling LGBT politics and education in the global South. *Curriculum Inquiry, 43*(4), 483–511.

Creswell, J. W., & Poth, C. N. (2018). *Qualitative inquiry & research design: Choosing among five approaches* (4th ed.). Sage.

Cruz, C. (2012). Making curriculum from scratch: Testimonio in an urban classroom. *Equity and Excellence in Education, 45*(3), 460–471.

Cruz-Malavé, A. (2007). *Queer Latino testimonio, Keith Haring, and Juanito xtravaganza*. Palgrave Macmillan.

Decena, C. U. (2011). *Tacit subjects: Belonging and same-sex desire among Dominican immigrant men*. Duke University Press.

DeLeon, A. P. (2010). How do I begin to tell a story that has not been told? Anarchism, autoethnography, and the middle ground. *Equity & Excellence in Education, 43*, 398–413.

Domínguez-Ruvalcaba, H. (2016). *Translating the queer: Body politics and transnational conversations*. Zed Books Ltd.

Domínguez-Ruvalcaba, H. (2019). *Latinoamérica queer: Cuerpo y política queer en América Latina*. Ariel.

Donoghue, M. E. (2014). *Borderland on the isthmus: Race, culture, and the struggle for the canal zone*. Duke University Press.

Falconi Trávez, D., Castellanos, S., & Viteri, M. A. (2014). *Resentir lo queer en América Latina: Diálogos desde el Sur*. Spain. Editorial Egales.

Fonseca Mora, R. (1997). *Soñar con la ciudad*. Santillana, S.A.

Fonseca Mora, R. (2001). *Soñar con la ciudad*. Santillana, S.A.

Glense, C. (2006). *Qualitative researchers: An introduction* (3rd ed.). Pearson.

González, R. (1996). *Muy macho: Latino men confront their manhood*. Anchor Books.

González, R. (2006). *Butterfly boy: Memories of a Chicano mariposa*. The University of Wisconsin Press.

Greetz, C. (1973). *The interpretation of cultures*. Basic Books.

Hames-Garcia, M. (2014a). *Gay Latino studies: A critical reader*. Duke University Press.

Hames-Garcia, M. (2014b). Joteria studies, or the political is personal. *Aztlan: A Journal of Chicano Studies, 39*(2), 135–141.

Hames-Garcia, M. R., & Martínez, E. J. (2011). *Gay Latino studies: A critical reader*. Duke University Press.

Holman Jones, S., Adams, T., & Ellis, C. (2013). Coming to know autoethnography as more than a method (pp. 17–47). In S. Holman Jones, T. E. Adams, & C. Ellis (Eds.), *Handbook of autoethnography*. Routledge.

Kempe, F. (1990). *Divorcing the dictator: America's bungled affair with Noriega.* G. P. Putnam's Sons.

Koster, R. M., & Sanchez, G. (1990). *In the time of the tyrants: Panama: 1968–1990.* W. W. Norton & Company, Inc.

Kumashiro, K. K. (2001). *Troubling intersections of race and sexuality: Queer students of color and anti-oppressive education.* Rowman & Littlefield.

Lemebel, P. (2020). Háblame de amores. Editorial Planeta Colombiana, S.A.

Madison, S. (1998). Performance, personal narratives, and the politics of possibility: The future of performance studies. In S. J. Dailey (Ed.), *The future of performance studies: Visions and revisions* (pp. 276–286). National Communication Association.

Manrique, J. (1999). *Eminent maricones: Arenas, Lorca, Puig and me.* University of Wisconsin Press.

McGuinness, A. (2003). Searching for "Latin America": Race and sovereignty in the Americas in the 1850s. In N. P. Appelbaum, A. S. Macpherson, & K. A. Rosemblatt (Eds.), *Race & nation in modern Latin America* (pp. 87–107). The University of North Carolina Press.

Mignolo, W. D. (2005). *The idea of Latin America.* Blackwell.

Mirandé, A. (1997). *Hombres y machos: Masculinity and Latino culture.* Westview Press.

Montenegro, E. (2022). Diagnostico sobre casos de discriminacion y mala praxis en la atención en servicios de salud a poblaciones claves y vulnerables a las ITS y VIH en Panamá. In O. Beluche & A. Carrera (Eds.), *Memoria del XVII congreso nacional de sociología,* Panamá, 9–12 de diciembre de 2021.

Muñoz, J. E. (1999). *Disidentifications: Queers of color and the performance of politics.* University of Minnesota Press.

Noriega, R. (2021, February 13). Las heroínas del silencio: Así se destapó el escándalo de abuso en los albergues. https://www.prensa.com/impresa/panorama/las-heroinas-del-silencio/

Ocampo, A. C. (2012). Making masculinity: Negotiations of gender presentation among Latino gay men. *Latino Studies, 10*(4), 448–472.

Pantoja Guzmán, O. (2021). In my Latinx gay shoes: Work, discrimination, immigration, and polyamory. In E. Rodríguez-Doranz (Ed.), *The everyday lives of gay men* (pp. 123–132). Routledge.

Palevi Gómez, A. (2016). Travestis, marimachas y maricones: El camino del arcoíris en El Salvador. *Revista Punto Género, 6.*

Peña, S. (2013). *Oye loca: From the Mariel boatlift to gay Cuban Miami.* University of Minnesota Press.

Perez, D. E. (2014). Toward a mariposa consciousness: Reimagining queer Chicano and Latino identities. *Aztlan: A Journal of Chicano Studies, 39*(2), 95–127.

Pernett y Morales, R. (2016). *Loma ardiente y vestida de sol.* Manfer, S.A.

Poulos, C. N. (2021). *Essentials of autoethnography.* American Psychological Association.

Pulido Ritter, L. (2005). *Recuerdo Panamá.* Articsa.

Quesada, U. (2015). *Queer brown voices. Personal narratives of Latina/o lgbt activism.* University of Texas Press.

Quiroga, J. (2000). *Tropics of desire: Interventions from queer Latino America.* New York University Press.

Ríos Vega, J. (2015). *Counter storytelling narratives of Latino teenage boys: From "vergüenza" to "échale ganas."* New York, N.Y.: Peter Lang Publishing.

Ríos Vega, J. (2017a). An unhealed wound: Growing up gay in Panama. *The Bilingual Review/La Revista Bilingüe, 33*(4), 76–79.

Ríos Vega, J. (2017b). La conciencia de la mariposa transnacional para entender la homosexualidad en Panamá. *Revista Convivencia, 3,* 81–108. http://up-rid.up.ac.pa/3714/1/2131

Ríos Vega, J. (2018). *Historias desde el sexilio.* Impresora Pacífico, S.A.

Ríos Vega, J. (2020). *High school Latinx counternarratives: Experiences in school and post-graduation.* New York, N.Y.: Peter Lang Publishing.

Ríos Vega, J. (2020a). Una mariposa transnacional: Memorias desde el sexilio. *Cuadernos Nacionales, 26,* 28–53. https://doi.org/10.48204/j.cnacionales.n26a2

Ríos Vega, J. (2020b). Undocuqueer Latinx: Counterstorytelling narratives during and post-high school. *Handbook on promoting social justice in education.* Springer Nature Switzerland.

Ríos Vega, J. (2022). *Testimonios LGBTIQ+ de Panamá.* Amazon.

Rocha Cortez, D. J. (2019). *Crónicas de la ciudad: Cochones, lirismos, memorias.* Soma Editores.

Rocha Cortez, D. J. (2022). *Cartografía de espacios en fuga Managua 1968–1975.* Anamá Ediciones.

Rodríguez-Dorans, E. (2021). Testing proximity and intimacy: An everyday reappropriation of private and public space. In E. Rodríguez-Doranz (Ed.), *The everyday lives of gay men* (pp. 113–122). Routledge.

Rodriquez, J. M. (2003). *Queer latinidad: Identity practices, discursive spaces.* New York University Press.

Salas Fonseca, P. E. (2005). *La Madrid.* Obra de Teatro Sin Publicar.

Salas Fonseca, P. E. (2016). *Mi hijo varón.* Obra de Teatro Sin Publicar.

Saldaña, J., & Omasta, M. (2018). *Qualitative research: Analyzing life.* Sage.

Sánchez Baute, A. (2003). *Al diablo la maldita primavera.* Penguin Random House.

Sigal, P. (2003). *Infamous desire: Male homosexuality in colonial Latin America.* The University of Chicago Press.

Soberón Torchía, E., & Arango, A. A. (1979). *Pepita de marañón: (es más, el día de la lata).* Ediciones Instituto Nacional de Cultura.

Stanziola, J. (2013a). Casco Viejo walks: Performing Panama's 'other' sexual space(s). *Intervention: International Journal of Post-Colonial Studies, 17*(6), 866–878. https://doi.org/10.1080/1369801X.2014.998261

Stanziola, J. (2013b). *Hombres enlodados.* Editorial Mariano Arosemena: Panamá.

Stavans, I. (1996). The Latin phallus. In R. González (Ed.), *Muy Macho: Latino men confront their manhood* (pp. 143–164). Anchor Books.

Tijerina Revilla, A., & Santillana, J. M. (2014). Joteria identity and consciousness. *Aztlan: A Journal of Chicano Studies, 39*(2), 167–179.

Trexler, R. C. (1995). *Sex and conquest: Gendered violence, political order and the European conquest of the Americas.* Cornell University Press.

Tuhiwai Smith, L. (2002). *Decolonizing methodologies: Research and indigenous peoples.* New Palgrave.

Urrieta, L. (2003). Las identidades también lloran, identities also cry: Exploring the human side of indigenous Latino/a identities. *Educational Studies, 34*(2), 147–212.